Winter Essentials

D1511434

Winter Essentials is a collection of knits to give you your perfect winter wardrobe.

From relaxed cardigan coats to a cosy cabled wrap, here are 12 essential pieces to take you through to Spring and beyond.

The designs are created in my sumptuous alpaca silk and cashmerino blends, the super soft luxury tweed and my classic Donegal chunky tweed.

Winter Essentials

Basic information

The quantities of yarn are based on average requirements and are therefore approximate. It is essential to work to the stated tension and you should always knit a tension square before starting. If you have too many stitches to 10cm/4in your tension is tight and you should change to a larger needle. If there are too few stitches, your tension is loose and you should change to a smaller needle. We cannot accept responsibility for the finished product if any yarn other than the one specified is used. Instructions given are for the first size, with larger sizes in round brackets. Where only one figure or instruction is given this applies to all sizes.

Work all directions inside square brackets the number of times stated. See ball band for washing and pressing instructions.

STANDARD ABBREVIATIONS

alt = alternate
beg = beginning
cont = continue
dec = decrease
foll = following
inc = increase
k = knit
kfb = knit into front and back of st
m1 = make one st by picking up the loop lying between st just worked and next st and working into back of it
p = purl
pfb = purl into front and back of st
patt = pattern
psso = pass slipped st over
rem = remaining
rep = repeat
skpo = slip 1, knit 1, pass slipped stitch over
sl = slip
ssk = [sl 1 knitwise] twice, insert tip of left needle from left to right through front of both sts and k2tog
st(s) = stitch(es)
st st = stocking stitch
tbl = through back loop
tog = together
yf = yarn forward
yo = yarn over needle
yrn = yarn round needle

USA GLOSSARY

cast off = bind off
moss stitch = seed stitch
tension = gauge
stocking stitch = stockinette stitch
yarn forward, yarn over needle, or yarn round needle = yarn over

Etoile

Ariel

Odette

Jeanne

Estelle

Elise

Natalie

Charlotte

Winter Essentials

Patterns

Contents

Camille

Etoile

Mathilde

Ariel

Odette

Jeanne

Estelle

Adele

Elise

Thandie

Natalie

Charlotte

Camille

MEASUREMENTS

To fit bust

| 81–86 | 92–97 | 102–107 | cm |
| 32–34 | 36–38 | 40–42 | in |

FINISHED MEASUREMENTS

Bust

| 92 | 102 | 112 | cm |
| 36 | 40 | 44 | in |

Length

| 82 | 84 | 87 | cm |
| 32¼ | 33 | 34¼ | in |

Sleeve length

47cm/18½in for all sizes

MATERIALS

- 11(12:13) 100g hanks of Debbie Bliss Donegal Chunky Tweed in Fuchsia 23.
- Pair each of 6.50mm (US 10½) and 7mm (US 10½) knitting needles.
- 3 large and 2 medium buttons.

TENSIONS

12½ sts and 18½ rows to 10cm/4in square over st st using 6½mm (US 10½) needles and 14 sts and 17 rows to 10cm/4in over dmst using 7mm (US 10½) needles.

ABBREVIATIONS

dmst = double moss st.
s2togkpo = slip next 2 sts as if to k2tog, k1, then pass 2 slipped sts over so centre st lies on top.

Also see page 6.

TIPS

- Do not join in new yarn at front edges.
- When casting off at sleeve top, to produce a smooth slope slip the first st, work the next st and pass the slipped st over, then cast off the next st in the usual way.
- The garment shown was made using two UK needle sizes of which there are no direct US equivalents, please refer to Tension/Gauge to decide which US needle sizes to use.

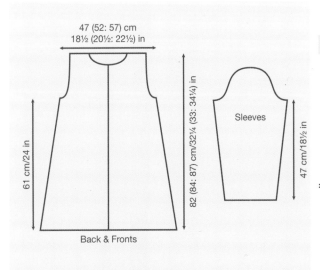

47 (52: 57) cm
18½ (20½: 22½) in

82 (84: 87) cm/32¼ (33: 34¼) in

61 cm/24 in

Sleeves

47 cm/18½ in

Back & Fronts

Camille

BACK

With 7mm (US 10½) needles, cast on 107(113:119) sts.
1st row (wrong side) K9(12:15), [p2, k1, p2, k9] 7 times, k0(3:6).
2nd row P9(12:15), [k2, p1, k2, p9] 7 times, p0(3:6).
3rd row K9(12:15), * [p1, k1] twice, p1, k9, rep from * 6 times more, k0(3:6).
4th row P9(12:15), *[k1, p1] twice, k1, p9, rep from * 6 times more, k0(3:6).
These 4 rows **form** panels of dmst outlined with one st in st st at each side and reverse st st between and at each side.
Patt 16 more rows.
1st dec row (wrong side) K9(12:15), [patt 5, k3, s2togkpo, k3] 6 times, patt 5, k9(12:15). 95(101:107) sts.
Cont in patt as now set and work 9 rows.
2nd dec row (wrong side) K1, k2tog, patt to last 3 sts, skpo, k1. 93(99:105) sts.
Cont in patt and dec in this way at each end of foll 10th row. 91(97:103) sts.
Patt 9 rows.
3rd dec row (wrong side) K1, k2tog, k4(7:10), [patt 5, k2, s2togkpo, k2] 6 times, patt 5, k4(7:10), skpo, k1. 77(83:89) sts.
Cont in patt and dec in same way as 2nd dec row at each end of 2 foll 10th rows. 73(79:85) sts.
Patt 9 rows.
4th dec row (wrong side) K1, k2tog, k1(4:7), [patt 5, k1, s2togkpo, k1] 6 times, patt 5, k1(4:7), skpo, k1. 59(65:71) sts.
Patt 11 rows, so ending with a right side row.
Change to 6½mm (US 10½) needles.
Yoke
K 3 rows.
Beg with a k row, work 18 rows in st st.
Shape armholes
Cast off 3(4:5) sts at beg of next 2 rows. 53(57:61) sts.
Dec row (right side) K1, k2tog, k to last 3 sts, skpo, k1. 51(55:59) sts.
Cont in st st and dec in this way at each end of next 4(5:6) right side rows. 43(45:47) sts.
Work 25(27:29) rows in st st.
Cast off.

LEFT FRONT

With 7mm (US 10½) needles, cast on 57(60:63) sts.
1st row (wrong side) [P1, k1] twice, p2, [k9, p2, k1, p2] 3 times, k9(12:15).
2nd row P9(12:15), [k2, p1, k2, p9] 3 times, k2, [p1, k1] twice.
3rd row [K1, p1] 3 times, * k9, [p1, k1] twice, p1, rep from * two times more, k9(12:15).
4th row P9(12:15), * [k1, p1] twice, k1, p9, rep from * two times more, [k1, p1] 3 times.
These 4 rows **form** panels of dmst outlined with one st in st st at each side with reverse st st between and at side

and with one st in st st and 5 sts in dmst for front band.
Patt 16 more rows.
1st dec row (wrong side) Patt 6, [k3, s2togkpo, k3, patt 5] 3 times, k9(12:15). 51(54:57) sts.
Cont in patt as now set and work 9 rows.
2nd dec row (wrong side) Patt to last 3 sts, skpo, k1. 50(53:56) sts.
Cont in patt and dec in this way at end of foll 10th row. 49(52:55) sts.
Patt 9 rows.
3rd dec row (wrong side), Patt 6, [k2, s2togkpo, k2, patt 5] 3 times, k4(7:10), k2tog, k1. 42(45:48) sts.
Cont in patt and dec in same way as 2nd dec row at end of 2 foll 10th rows. 40(43:46) sts.
Patt 9 rows.
4th dec row (wrong side) Patt 6, [k1, s2togkpo, k1, patt 5] 3 times, k1(4:7), k2tog, k1. 33(36:39) sts.
Patt 11 rows, so ending with a right side row.
Change to 6½mm (US 10½) needles.
Yoke
1st row (wrong side) Dmst 5, p1, k to end.
2nd row K to last 5 sts, dmst 5.
3rd row As 1st row.
4th row As 2nd row.
5th row Dmst 5, p to end.
4th and 5th rows form st st with 5 sts in dmst for front band.
Work 16 more rows.
Shape armhole
Cast off 3(4:5) sts at beg of next row. 30(32:34) sts.
Work 1 row.
Dec row (right side) K1, k2tog, k to last 5 sts, dmst 5. 29(31:33) sts.
Cont in patt and dec in this way at beg (armhole edge) of next 4(5:6) right side rows. 25(26:27) sts.
Patt 5 rows.
Shape neck
Next row (right side) K to last 9 sts, turn and leave these 9 sts on a holder for neckband and collar, cont on rem 16(17:18) sts.
P 1 row.
Dec row (right side) K to last 2 sts, skpo. 15(16:17) sts.
Cont in st-st dec in this way at end (neck edge) of next 4 right side rows. 11(12:13) sts.
Work 9(11:13) rows in st st.
Cast off.

RIGHT FRONT

With 7mm (US 10½) needles, cast on 57(60:63) sts.
1st row (wrong side) K9(12:15), [p2, k1, p2, k9] 3 times, p2, [k1, p1] twice.
2nd row [K1, p1] twice, k2, [p9, k2, p1, k2] 3 times, p9(12:15).

3rd row K9(12:15), * [p1, k1] twice, p1, k9, rep from * twice more, [p1, k1] 3 times.

4th row [K1, p1] 3 times, * p9, [k1, p1] twice, k1, rep from * two times more, p9(12:15).

These 4 rows **form** panels of dmst outlined with one st in st st at each side with reverse st st between and at side and with one st in st st and 5 sts in dmst for front band. Patt 16 more rows.

1st dec row (wrong side) P9(12:15), [patt 5, k3, s2togkpo, k3] 3 times, patt 6. 51(54:57) sts.

Cont in patt as now set and work 9 rows.

2nd dec row (wrong side) K1, k2tog, patt to end. 50(53:56) sts.

Cont in patt and dec in this way at beg of foll 10th row. 49(52:55) sts.

Patt 9 rows.

3rd dec row (wrong side) K1, k2tog, k4(7:10), [patt 5, k2, s2togkpo, k2] 3 times, patt 6. 42(45:48) sts.

Cont in patt and dec in same way as 2nd dec row at beg of 2 foll 10th rows. 40(43:46) sts.

Patt 9 rows.

4th dec row (wrong side) K1, k2tog, k1(4:7), [patt 5, k1, s2togkpo, k1] 3 times, patt 6. 33(36:39) sts.

Patt 11 rows, so ending with a right side row.

Change to 6½mm (US 10½) needles.

Yoke

1st row (wrong side) K to last 6 sts, p1, dmst 5.

1st buttonhole row K1, p2tog, yo, k2tog, k to end.

3rd row As 1st row but working p1, k1 into yo.

4th row Dmst 5, k to end.

5th row P to last 5 sts, dmst 5.

4th and 5th rows **form** st st with 5 sts in dmst for front band. Patt 16 more rows.

Make 2nd buttonhole on next row.

Shape armhole

Next row (wrong side) Cast off 3(4:5) sts, patt to end working p1, k1 into yo. 30(32:34) sts.

Dec row (right side) Dmst 5, k to last 3 sts, skpo, k1. 29(31:33) sts.

Cont in patt and dec in this way at end (armhole edge) of next 4(5:6) right side rows. 25(26:27) sts.

Patt 5 rows.

Shape neck

Next row (right side) Patt 9 and leave these 9 sts on a holder for neckband and collar, k to end. 16(17:18) sts.

P 1 row.

Dec row (right side) K2tog, k to end. 15(16:17) sts.

Cont in st st and dec in this way at beg (neck edge) of next 4 right side rows. 11(12:13) sts.

Work 9(11:13) rows in st st.

Cast off.

SLEEVES

With 6½mm (US 10½) needles, cast on 34(36:38) sts.

1st row (right side) [K1, p1] to end.

2nd row [P1, k1] to end.

3rd row [P1, k1] to end.

4th row [K1, p1] to end.

These 4 rows **form** dmst and are repeated.

Work 4 more rows.

Beg with a k row, work 18(10:10) rows in st st.

Inc row (right side) K1, kfb, k to last 3 sts, kfb, k2. 36(38:40) sts.

Cont in st st and inc in this way at each end of 5(7:9) foll 12th(10th:8th) rows. 46(52:58) sts.

Work 9(7:5) rows in st st.

Shape top

Cast off 3(4:5) sts at beg of next 2 rows. 40(44:48) sts.

Dec row (right side) K1, k2tog, k to last 3 sts, skpo, k1. 38(42:46) sts.

Cont in st st and dec in this way at each end of next 4(5:6) right side rows. 30(32:34) sts.

Work 5 rows in st st.

Dec as before at each end of next row and on 3 foll right side rows. 22(24:26) sts.

P 1 row.

Next row (right side) Cast off 2 sts, k to last 2 sts, skpo. 19(21:23) sts.

Next row Cast off 2 sts, p to last 2 sts, p2tog. 16(18:20) sts.

Work last 2 rows once again. 10(12:14) sts.

Cast off.

HALF BELT

With 6½mm (US 10½) needles, cast on 33 sts.

1st row (right side) P1, [k1, p1] to end.

2nd row K1, [p1, k1] to end.

3rd row K1, [p1, k1] to end.

4th row P1, [k1, p1] to end.

5th row P1, [k1, p1] to end.

Cast off in dmst.

COLLAR

Matching sts, join shoulders.

With 6½mm (US 10½) needles, slip 9 sts from right front holder onto needle, pick up and k21(23:25) sts up right front neck, 23 sts across back neck and 21(23:25) sts down left front neck, patt 9 sts from holder. 83(87:91) sts.

Working in patt as set by front neck sts, work 3 rows in dmst.

Make 3rd buttonhole on next row.
Working p1, k1 into yo, dmst one more row.
Next row Cast off 4 sts in patt, dmst to last 4 sts,
cast off 4 sts in patt. 75(79:83) sts.
Turn, rejoin yarn and work 15 rows in dmst.
Cast off loosely in patt.

TO MAKE UP

Sew sleeves into armholes, easing to fit. Join side
and sleeve seams, reversing seam for turn back.
Sew on buttons. Place half belt on centre back at
lower edge of yoke, and stitch in place with buttons.

Etoile

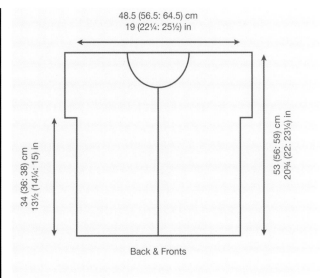

48.5 (56.5: 64.5) cm
19 (22¼: 25½) in

34 (36: 38) cm
13½ (14¼: 15) in

53 (56: 59) cm
20¾ (22: 23¼) in

Back & Fronts

MEASUREMENTS

To fit bust

81–92	97–107	112–122	cm
32–36	38–42	44–48	in

FINISHED MEASUREMENTS

Bust

99	115	131	cm
39	45¼	51½	in

Length to shoulder

53	56	59	cm
20¾	22	23¼	in

MATERIALS

- 11(12:13) 50g balls of Debbie Bliss cashmerino aran in Camel 29.
- Pair each 4.50mm (US 7) and 5mm (US 8) knitting needles.
- Cable needle.
- 4 buttons.

TENSION

30 sts and 28 rows to 10cm/4in square over 4-st cable patt using 5mm (US 8) needles.

ABBREVIATIONS

C4B = slip next 2 sts onto cable needle and hold at back of work, k2, then k2 from cable needle.
C4F = slip next 2 sts onto cable needle and hold to front of work, k2, then k2 from cable needle.

Also see page 6.

BACK

With 5mm (US 8) needles, cast on 146(170:194) sts.
1st row (right side) P2, [k4, p2] to end.
2nd row K2, [p4, k2] to end.
3rd row P2, [C4B, p2] 12(14:16) times, [C4F, p2] 12(14:16) times.
4th row As 2nd row.
These 4 rows **form** the cable patt and are repeated until back measures 31(33:35)cm/12¼(13:13¾)in from cast on edge, ending with a 3rd row.
Yoke dec row (wrong side) [K2, p2tog tbl, p2tog tbl] 11(13:15) times, k2, [p4, k2] twice, [p2tog, p2tog, k2] 11(13:15) times. 102(118:134) sts.
Now work in patt as follows:
1st row (right side) P2, [k2, p2] 11(13:15) times, [k4, p2] twice, [k2, p2] 11(13:15) times.
2nd row K1, [p2, k2] 11(13:15) times, k1, p4, k2, p4, k1, [k2, p2] 11(13:15) times, k1.
3rd row P1, [k2, p2] 11(13:15) times, p1, C4B, p2, C4F, p1, [p2, k2] 11(13:15) times, p1.
4th row [P2, k2] 11(13:15) times, p1, k1, p4, k2, p4, k1, p1, [k2, p2] 11(13:15) times.
5th row [K2, p2] 11(13:15) times, k1, p1, k4, p2, k4, p1, k1, [p2, k2] 11(13:15) times.
6th row P1, [k2, p2] 11(13:15) times, k1, p4, k2, p4, k1, [p2, k2] 11(13:15) times, p1.
7th row K1, [p2, k2] 11(13:15) times, p1, C4B, p2, C4F, p1, [k2, p2] 11(13:15) times, k1.
8th row K2, [p2, k2] 11(13:15) times, [p4, k2] twice, [p2, k2] 11(13:15) times.
These 8 rows **form** the patt.

Shape for armholes

Next row (right side) Cast on 11 sts and work: k1, [p1, k1] 3 times, p2, k2 across these sts, patt to end as 1st row.
Next row Cast on 11 sts and work: k1, [p1, k1] 3 times, k1, p2, k1 across these sts, patt to last 7 sts, [k1, p1] 3 times, k1. 124(140:156) sts.
These 2 rows **re-set** the patt with 4 sts in patt and 7 sts in moss st worked at each end.
Cont in patt as now set until back measures 53(56:59)cm/20 3/4(22:23¼)in from cast on edge, measured in the centre and ending with a 7th patt row.
Next row (wrong side) Cast off 40(48:56) sts, with one st on needle after cast off, patt next 43 sts, cast off rem 40(48:56) sts.
Leave rem 44 sts in centre on a holder for collar.

LEFT FRONT

With 5mm (US 8) needles, cast on 78(90:102) sts.
1st row (right side) [P2, k4] 12(14:16) times, [p1, k1] 3 times.
2nd row K1, [p1, k1] twice, k1, [p4, k2] to end.
3rd row [P2, C4B] 12(14:16) times, [p1, k1] 3 times.

4th row As 2nd row.
These 4 rows **form** the cable patt with moss st front edge and are repeated until front measures 31(33:35)cm/12¼(13:13¾)in from cast on edge, ending with a 3rd row.
Yoke dec row (wrong side) K1, [p1, k1] twice, k1, p4, k2, [p2tog, p2tog, k2] to end. 56(64:72) sts.
Now work in patt as follows:
1st row (right side) [P2, k2] 11(13:15) times, p2, k4, [p1, k1] 3 times.
2nd row K1, [p1, k1] twice, k1, p4, k1, [k2, p2] 11(13:15) times, k1.
3rd row P1, [k2, p2] 11(13:15) times, p1, C4B, [p1, k1] 3 times.
4th row K1, [p1, k1] twice, k1, p4, k1, p1, [k2, p2] 11(13:15) times.
5th row [K2, p2] 11(13:15) times, k1, p1, k4, [p1, k1] 3 times.
6th row K1, [p1, k1] twice, k1, p4, k1, [p2, k2] 11(13:15) times, p1.
7th row K1, [p2, k2] 11(13:15) times, p1, C4B, [p1, k1] 3 times.
8th row K1, [p1, k1] twice, k1, p4, k2, [p2, k2] 11(13:15) times.
These 8 rows **form** the patt.

Shape for armhole

Next row (right side) Cast on 11 sts and work: k1, [p1, k1] 3 times, p2, k2 across these sts, patt to end as 1st row. 67(75:83) sts.
This row **re-sets** the patt with 4 sts in patt and 7 sts at armhole edge worked in moss st.
Cont in patt as now set until front measures 47(50:53)cm/18½(19¾:20¾)in from cast on edge, measured along the 4-st cable and ending with a 4th patt row.

Shape neck

Next row (right side) Patt to last 11 sts, turn and leave 11 sts at centre front on a holder, cont on rem 56(64:72) sts.
Keeping patt correct throughout, cast off 4 sts at beg (neck edge) of next row, 3 sts at beg of foll 2 wrong side rows and 2 sts at beg of next 3 wrong side rows.
Work straight in patt for a few rows until front measures same as Back to shoulder, ending at armhole edge.
Cast off in patt.
Mark the position for 3 buttons, the first to be worked on the 1st(3rd:5th) row after yoke dec row and the 3rd, just below neck shaping.

RIGHT FRONT

Buttonhole row (right side) K1, p1, k1, yf, k2tog, patt to end.
With 5mm (US 8) needles, cast on 78(90:102) sts.
1st row (right side) [K1, p1] 3 times, [k4, p2] 12(14:16) times.

2nd row [K2, p4] 12(14:16) times, k2, [p1, k1] twice.

3rd row [K1, p1] 3 times, [C4F, p2] 12(14:16) times.

4th row As 2nd row.

These 4 rows **form** the cable patt with moss st front edge and are repeated until front measures 31(33:35)cm/ 12¼(13:13¾)in from cast on edge, ending with a 3rd row.

Yoke dec row (wrong side) [K2, p2tog, p2tog] 11(13:15) times, k2, p4, k2, [p1, k1] twice. 56(64:72) sts.

Now work in patt as follows (working buttonholes to match markers as given):

1st row (right side) [K1, p1] 3 times, k4, p2, [k2, p2] to end.

2nd row K1, [p2, k2] 11(13:15) times, k1, p4, k1, [k1, p1] twice, k1.

3rd row [K1, p1] 3 times, C4F, p1, [p2, k2] 11(13:15) times, p1.

4th row [P2, k2] 11(13:15) times, p1, k1, p4, k1, [k1, p1] twice, k1.

5th row [K1, p1] 3 times, k4, p1, k1, [p2, k2] 11(13:15) times.

6th row P1, [k2, p2] 11(13:15) times, k1, p4, k1, [k1, p1] twice, k1.

7th row [K1, p1] 3 times, C4F, p1, [k2, p2] 11(13:15) times, k1.

8th row [K2, p2] 11(13:15) times, k2, p4, k1, [k1, p1] twice, k1.

These 8 rows **form** the patt.

Work 1st row once more.

Shape for armhole

Next row (wrong side) Cast on 11 sts and work: k1, [p1, k1] 3 times, k1, p2, k1 across these sts, patt to end as 2nd row. 67(75:83) sts.

This row **re-sets** the patt with 4 sts in patt and 7 sts at armhole edge worked in moss st.

Cont in patt as now set until front measures 47(50:53)cm/ 18½(19¾:20¾)in from cast on edge, measured along the 4-st cable and ending with a 4th patt row.

Shape neck

Next row (right side) Patt 11 sts and slip these sts onto a holder for collar, patt to end. 56(64:72) sts.

Patt 1 row.

Keeping patt correct throughout, cast off 4 sts at beg (neck edge) of next row, 3 sts at beg of foll 2 right side rows and 2 sts at beg of next 3 right side rows.

Work straight in patt for a few rows until front measures same as Back to shoulder, ending at armhole edge.

Cast off in patt.

COLLAR

Join shoulder seams.

With right side facing and 4.50mm (US 7) needles, slip 11 sts on right front holder onto needle, rejoin yarn and pick up and k24 sts up right front neck, work: p1, [k2, p2] 4 times,

k4, p2, k4, [p2, k2] 4 times, p1 across 44 sts on back neck holder, pick up and k24 sts down left front neck, then work: p1, k4, [p1, k1] 3 times across 11 sts on left front holder. 114 sts.

1st row (wrong side) [K1, p1] twice, k2, p4, k1, [p2, k2] 9 times, p2, k3, p4, k2, p4, k3, p2, [k2, p2] 9 times, k1, p4, k2, [p1, k1] twice.

2nd row [K1, p1] 3 times, C4F, p1, [k2, p2] 10 times, p1, C4B, p2, C4F, p1, [p2, k2] 10 times, p1, C4B, [p1, k1] 3 times.

3rd row As 1st row.

4th row [K1, p1] 3 times, k4, p1, [k2, p2] 10 times, p1, k4, p2, k4, p1, [p2, k2] 10 times, p1, k4, [p1, k1] 3 times.

These 4 rows **form** the collar patt and are repeated twice more.

Patt 3 rows.

Buttonhole row K1, p1, k1, yf, k2tog, p1, k4, p1, [k2, p2] 10 times, p1, k4, p2, k4, p1, [p2, k2] 10 times, p1, k4, [p1, k1] 3 times.

Patt 3 rows.

Next row (right side) Cast off in patt, but work purl across first and last cables and work [p2tog] twice, p2, [p2tog tbl] twice over centre 10 sts.

TO MAKE UP

Join side and underarm seams. Sew on buttons.

Mathilde

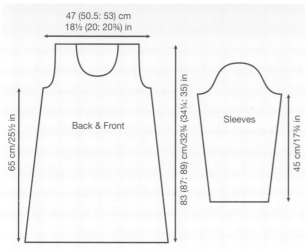

47 (50.5: 53) cm
18½ (20: 20¾) in

Back & Front

65 cm/25½ in

83 (87: 89) cm/32¾ (34¼: 35) in

Sleeves

45 cm/17¾ in

MEASUREMENTS

To fit bust

81–86	86–92	92–97	cm
32–34	34–36	36–38	in

FINISHED MEASUREMENTS

Bust

94	101	106	cm
37	39¾	41¾	in

Length

83	87	89	cm
32¾	34¼	35	in

Sleeve

45cm/17¾in for all sizes

MATERIALS

- 19(20:21) 50g balls of Debbie Bliss cashmerino dk in Charcoal 34.
- Pair of 4mm (US 6) knitting needles.
- 4mm (US 6) circular needle (see Tips).
- Cable needle.
- 60cm length 3.75mm (US 5) and 4mm (US 6) circular needle.

TENSION

24 sts and 30 rows to 10cm/4in square over rib, when slightly stretched using 4mm (US 6) needles.

ABBREVIATIONS

C3B = slip next st onto cable needle, hold at back of work, k2, then k1 from cable needle.
C3BP = slip next st onto cable needle, hold at back of work, k2, then p1 from cable needle.
C3F = slip next 2 sts onto cable needle, hold to front of work, k1, then k2 from cable needle.
C3FP = slip next 2 sts onto cable needle, hold to front of work, p1, then k2 from cable needle.
C4B = slip next 2 sts onto cable needle, hold at back of work, k2, then k2 from cable needle.
C4F = slip next 2 sts onto cable needle, hold to front of work, k2, then k2 from cable needle.
m1 pwise = make one st by picking up and purling into back of loop lying between st just worked and next st.

Also see page 6.

TIPS

- When working the lower edge of the back and front, you may need to use a 4mm (US 6) circular needle.
- When picking up sts across the back neck, where necessary, pick up two sts from each side of a single purl st and pick up only 2 sts from the 4-st cables to make the rib relate smoothly to the pattern.
- For a shorter dress, omit the 2nd repeat of the 18-st diamond panel. Your dress will be approximately 10cm/4in shorter and you will need 2 less balls of yarn.

PANEL A

Worked over 12 sts.
1st row (right side) K2, p2, C4B, p2, k2.
2nd row P2, k2, p4, k2, p2.
3rd row K2, p2, k4, p2, k2.
4th row As 2nd row.
These 4 rows **form** the cable and rope cable panel patt and are repeated.

BACK

With 4mm (US 6) needles, cast on 246(262:278) sts.
1st row (right side) K2, [p2, k2] to end.
2nd row P2, [k2, p2] to end.
These 2 rows **form** rib and are repeated.
Rib 4 more rows.
1st set up row (right side) [K2, p6] 2(3:4) times, [k2, p2, k1, skpo, k2tog, k1, p2, k2, p10, C3FP, C3BP, p10] 5 times, k2, p2, k1, skpo, k2tog, k1, p2, k2, [p6, k2] 2(3:4) times. 234(250:266) sts.
2nd set up row (wrong side) [P2, k6] 2(3:4) times, [p2, k2, p4, k2, p2, k11, p4, k11] 5 times, p2, k2, p4, k2, p2, [k6, p2] 2(3:4) times.
These 2 rows **set** the position of five 26-st diamond cable panels and six 12-st rib and rope cable panels with 2(3:4) panels of p6 and k2 rib at each side.
Now work in patt as follows:
1st row (right side) Rib 16(24:32), [work 12 sts of 1st row of panel A, p11, C4F, p11] 5 times, work 12 sts of 1st row of panel A, rib 16(24:32).
2nd and every wrong side row K and p the sts as they appear.
3rd row Rib 16(24:32), [patt 12 (3rd row panel A), p10, C3B, C3F, p10] 5 times, patt 12 (3rd row panel A), rib 16(24:32).
5th row Rib 16(24:32), [patt 12 (1st row panel A), p9, C3B, k2, C3F, p9] 5 times, patt 12 (1st row panel A), rib 16(24:32).
7th row Rib 16(24:32), [patt 12, p8, C3BP, C4B, C3FP, p8] 5 times, patt 12, rib 16(24:32).
9th row Rib 16(24:32), [patt 12, p7, C3BP, p1, k4, p1, C3FP, p7] 5 times, patt 12, rib 16(24:32).
11th row Rib 16(24:32), [patt 12, p6, C3BP, p2, C4B, p2, C3FP, p6] 5 times, patt 12, rib 16(24:32).
13th row Rib 16(24:32), [patt 12, p5, C3BP, p3, k4, p3, C3FP, p5] 5 times, patt 12, rib 16(24:32).
15th row Rib 16(24:32), [patt 12, p4, C3BP, p4, C4B, p4, C3FP, p4] 5 times, patt 12, rib 16(24:32).
17th row Rib 16(24:32), [patt 12, p3, C3BP, p5, k4, p5, C3FP, p3] 5 times, patt 12, rib 16(24:32).
19th row Rib 16(24:32), [patt 12, p2, C3BP, p6, C4B, p6, C3FP, p2] 5 times, patt 12, rib 16(24:32).

21st row Rib 16(24:32), [patt 12, p1, C3BP, p7, k4, p7, C3FP, p1] 5 times, patt 12, rib 16(24:32).
23rd row Rib 16(24:32), [patt 12, p1, k2, p8, C4B, p8, k2, p1] 5 times, patt 12, rib 16(24:32).
25th row Rib 16(24:32), [patt 12, p1, C3FP, p7, k4, p7, C3BP, p1] 5 times, patt 12, rib 16(24:32).
27th row Rib 16(24:32), [patt 12, p2, C3FP, p6, C4B, p6, C3BP, p2] 5 times, patt 12, rib 16(24:32).
29th row Rib 16(24:32), [patt 12, p3, C3FP, p5, k4, p5, C3BP p, p3] 5 times, patt 12, rib 16(24:32).
31st row Rib 16(24:32), [patt 12, p4, C3FP, p4, C4B, p4, C3BP, p4] 5 times, patt 12, rib 16(24:32).
33rd row Rib 16(24:32), [patt 12, p5, C3FP, p3, k4, p3, C3BP, p5] 5 times, patt 12, rib 16(24:32).
35th row Rib 16(24:32), [patt 12, p6, C3FP, p2, C4B, p2, C3BP, p6] 5 times, patt 12, rib 16(24:32).
37th row Rib 16(24:32), [patt 12, p7, C3FP, p1, k4, p1, C3BP, p7] 5 times, patt 12, rib 16(24:32).
39th row Rib 16(24:32), [patt 12, p8, C3FP, C4B, C3BP, p8] 5 times, patt 12, rib 16(24:32).
41st row Rib 16(24:32), [patt 12, p9, C3FP, k2, C3BP, p9] 5 times, patt 12, rib 16(24:32).
43rd row Rib 16(24:32), [patt 12, p10, C3FP, C3BP, p10] 5 times, patt 12, rib 16(24:32).
45th and 46th rows As 1st and 2nd rows.
26-st diamond panel is now complete.
47th row Rib 16(24:32), [patt 12, p9, slip next 2 sts onto cable needle, hold at back, k2, then k2tog from cable needle, slip next 2 sts onto cable needle, hold to front, skpo, then k2 from cable needle, p9] 5 times, patt 12, rib 16(24:32). 224(240:256) sts.
49th row Rib 16(24:32), [patt 12, p7, slip next 2 sts onto cable needle, hold at back, k2, then k2tog from cable needle, k2, slip next 2 sts onto cable needle, hold to front, skpo, then k2 from cable needle, p7] 5 times, patt 12, rib 16(24:32). 214(230:246) sts.
51st row Rib 16(24:32), [patt 12, p6, C3BP, C4B, C3FP, p6] 5 times, patt 12, rib 16(24:32).
53rd row Rib 16(24:32), [patt 12, p5, C3BP, p1, k4, p1, C3FP, p5] 5 times, patt 12, rib 16(24:32).
55th row Rib 16(24:32), [patt 12, p4, C3BP, p2, C4B, p2, C3FP, p4] 5 times, patt 12, rib 16(24:32).
57th row Rib 16(24:32), [patt 12, p3, C3BP, p3, k4, p3, C3FP, p3] 5 times, patt 12, rib 16(24:32).
59th row Rib 16(24:32), [patt 12, p2, C3BP, p4, C4B, p4, C3FP, p2] 5 times, patt 12, rib 16(24:32).
61st row Rib 16(24:32), [patt 12, p1, C3BP, p5, k4, p5, C3FP, p1] 5 times, patt 12, rib 16(24:32).
63rd row Rib 16(24:32), [patt 12, p1, k2, p6, C4B, p6, k2, p1] 5 times, patt 12, rib 16(24:32).
65th row Rib 16(24:32), [patt 12, p1, C3FP, p5, k4, p5, C3BP, p1] 5 times, patt 12, rib 16(24:32).

67th row Rib 16(24:32), [patt 12, p2, C3FP, p4, C4B, p4, C3BP, p2] 5 times, patt 12, rib 16(24:32).

69th row Rib 16(24:32), [patt 12, p3, C3FP, p3, k4, p3, C3BP, p3] 5 times, patt 12, rib 16(24:32).

71st row Rib 16(24:32), [patt 12, p4, C3FP, p2, C4B, p2, C3BP, p4] 5 times, patt 12, rib 16(24:32).

73rd row Rib 16(24:32), [patt 12, p5, C3FP, p1, k4, p1, C3BP, p5] 5 times, patt 12, rib 16(24:32).

75th row Rib 16(24:32), [patt 12, p6, C3FP, C4B, C3BP, p6] 5 times, patt 12, rib 16(24:32).

77th row Rib 16(24:32), [patt 12, p7, C3FP, k2, C3BP, p7] 5 times, patt 12, rib 16(24:32).

79th row Rib 16(24:32), [patt 12, p8, C3FP, C3BP, p8] 5 times, patt 12, rib 16(24:32).

81st row Rib 16(24:32), [patt 12, p9, c4f, p9] 5 times, patt 12, rib 16(24:32).

22-st diamond panel is now complete.

82nd row (wrong side) [P2, skpo, k2, k2tog] 2(3:4) times, patt to last 16(24:32) sts, [skpo, k2, k2tog, p2] 2(3:4) times. 206(218:230) sts.

83rd row Rib 12(18:24), [patt 12, p7, slip next 2 sts onto cable needle, hold at back, k2, then k2tog from cable needle, slip next 2 sts onto cable needle, hold to front, skpo, then k2 from cable needle, p7] 5 times, patt 12, rib 12(18:24). 196(208:220) sts.

85th row Rib 12(18:24), [patt 12, p5, slip next 2 sts onto cable needle, hold at back, k2, then k2tog from cable needle, k2, slip next 2 sts onto cable needle, hold to front, skpo, then k2 from cable needle, p5] 5 times, patt 12, rib 12(18:24). 186(198:210) sts

87th row Rib 12(18:24), [patt 12, p4, C3BP, C4B, C3FP, p4] 5 times, patt 12, rib 12(18:24).

89th row Rib 12(18:24), [patt 12, p3, C3BP, p1, k4, p1, C3FP, p3] 5 times, patt 12, rib 12(18:24).

91st row Rib 12(18:24), [patt 12, p2, C3BP, p2, C4B, p2, C3FP, p2] 5 times, patt 12, rib 12(18:24).

93rd row Rib 12(18:24), [patt 12, p1, C3BP, p3, k4, p3, C3FP, p1] 5 times, patt 12, rib 12(18:24).

95th row Rib 12(18:24), [patt 12, p1, k2, p4, C4B, p4, k2, p1] 5 times, patt 12, rib 12(18:24).

97th row Rib 12(18:24), [patt 12, p1, C3FP, p3, k4, p3, C3BP, p1] 5 times, patt 12, rib 12(18:24).

99th row Rib 12(18:24), [patt 12, p2, C3FP, p2, C4B, p2, C3BP, p2] 5 times, patt 12, rib 12(18:24).

101st row Rib 12(18:24), [patt 12, p3, C3FP, p1, k4, p1, C3BP, p3] 5 times, patt 12, rib 12(18:24).

103rd row Rib 12(18:24), [patt 12, p4, C3FP, C4B, C3BP, p4] 5 times, patt 12, rib 12(18:24).

105th row Rib 12(18:24), [patt 12, p5, C3FP, k2, C3BP, p5] 5 times, patt 12, rib 12(18:24).

107th row Rib 12(18:24), [patt 12, p6, C3FP, C3BP, p6] 5 times, patt 12, rib 12(18:24).

109th row Rib 12(18:24), [patt 12, p7, C4F, p7] 5 times, patt 12, rib 12(18:24).

First line of 18-st diamond panels is now complete.

111th row Rib 12(18:24), [patt 12, p6, C3B, C3F, p6] 5 times, patt 12, rib 12(18:24).

113th row Rib 12(18:24), [patt 12, p5, C3B, k2, C3F, p5] 5 times, patt 12, rib 12(18:24).

115th to 137th rows Work as given for 87th to 109th rows. 2nd line of 18-st diamond panels is now complete.

138th row (wrong side) [P2, skpo, k2tog] 2(3:4) times, patt to last 12 sts, [skpo, k2tog, p2] 2(3:4) times. 178(186:194) sts.

139th row Rib 8(12:16), [patt 12, p5, slip next 2 sts onto cable needle, hold at back, k2, then k2tog from cable needle, slip next 2 sts onto cable needle, hold to front, skpo, then k2 from cable needle, p5] 5 times, patt 12, rib 8(12:16). 168(176:184) sts.

141st row Rib 8(12:16), [patt 12, p3, slip next 2 sts onto cable needle, hold at back, k2, then k2tog from cable needle, k2, slip next 2 sts onto cable needle, hold to front, skpo, then k2 from cable needle, p3] 5 times, patt 12, rib 8(12:16). 158(166:174) sts.

143rd row Rib 8(12:16), [patt 12, p2, C3BP, C4B, C3FP, p2] 5 times, patt 12, rib 8(12:16).

145th row Rib 8(12:16), [patt 12, p1, C3BP, p1, k4, p1, C3FP, p1] 5 times, patt 12, rib 8(12:16).

147th row Rib 8(12:16), [patt 12, p1, k2, p2, C4B, p2, k2, p1] 5 times, patt 12, rib 8(12:16).

149th row Rib 8(12:16), [patt 12, p1, C3FP, p1, k4, p1, C3BP, p1] 5 times, patt 12, rib 8(12:16).

151st row Rib 8(12:16), [patt 12, p2, C3FP, C4B, C3BP, p2] 5 times, patt 12, rib 8(12:16).

153rd row Rib 8(12:16), [patt 12, p3, C3FP, k2, C3BP, p3] 5 times, patt 12, rib 8(12:16).

155th row Rib 8(12:16), [patt 12, p4, C3FP, C3BP, p4] 5 times, patt 12, rib 8(12:16).

157th row Rib 8(12:16), [patt 12, p5, C4F, p5] 5 times, patt 12, rib 8(12:16).

159th row Rib 8(12:16), [patt 12, p4, C3F, C3B, p4] 5 times, patt 12, rib 8(12:16).

161st row Rib 8(12:16), [patt 12, p3, C3F, k2, C3B, p3] 5 times, patt 12, rib 8(12:16).

141st to 162nd rows **form** the 14-st small diamond panel patt with rib and rope cables between and 2 x 2 rib at each side.

Patt 10 more rows.

Shape armholes

Cast off 6 sts at beg of next 2 rows. 146(154:162) sts **.

Working k2tog, skpo, or p2tog as necessary to keep rib correct, dec one st at each end of next 11 right side rows. 124(132:140) sts.

Patt 31(41:47) rows.

Decreasing over cables, cast off.

FRONT

Work as given for Back to **.
Dec one st at each end of next 1(6:6) right side rows.
144(142:150) sts.
Patt 1 row.

Shape left side of neck

1st row (right side) K2tog, patt until there are 43(42:46) sts on right needle, turn and complete left side on these sts.
[Cast off 2 sts at beg of next row and dec one st at each end of foll row] 4 times.
Cast off 2 sts at beg of next row. 25(24:28) sts.
1st size only Dec at armhole edge only on next 5 right side rows.
All sizes 20(24:28) sts.
Patt 31(41:47) rows.
Cast off.

Shape right side of neck

1st row With right side facing, slip 56 sts at centre front onto a holder, patt to last 2 sts, skpo. 43(42:46) sts.
[Dec one st at end of next row and cast off 2 sts at beg and dec one st at end of foll row] 4 times.
1st size only Dec one st at end of next row, then dec one st at each end of foll row.
Patt one row.
Dec 1 st at end of next row and 3 foll right side rows.
2nd and 3rd sizes only Dec one st at beg of next row and foll right side row.
All sizes 20(24:28) sts.
Patt 31(39:45) rows.
Cast off.

SLEEVES

With 4mm (US 6) needles, cast on 62 sts.
1st row (right side) K2, [p2, k2] to end.
2nd row P2, [k2, p2] to end.
These 2 rows form rib.
Rib 30(8:14) more rows.
Inc row (right side) K2, m1, rib to last 2 sts, m1, k2. 64 sts.
Taking inc sts into rib, inc in this way at each end of 11(15:19) foll 8th(8th:6th) rows. 86(94:102) sts.
Rib 17(7:7) rows.

Shape top

Cast off 6 sts at beg of next 2 rows. 74(82:90) sts.
Next row (right side) K2tog, rib to last 2 sts, skpo. 72(80:88) sts.
Next row P3, rib to last 3 sts, p3.
Dec row (right side) K2, skpo, rib to last 4 sts, k2tog, k2. 70(78:86) sts.
Rep the last 2 rows 11 times more. 48(56:64) sts.
Rib 1 row.
Next row (right side) K2tog, rib to last 2 sts, skpo. 46(54:62) sts.

Cont in rib, dec in this way at each end of next right side row. 44(52:60) sts.
P2tog at each end of next 2 right side rows. 40(48:56) sts.
Work 1 row.
Cast off 2 sts at beg and dec one st at end of next 4 rows. 28(36:44) sts.
Cast off.

NECKBAND

Matching sts, join shoulders. With 3.75mm (US 5) circular needle, pick up and k one st from right shoulder seam, 76 sts across back neck, one st from left shoulder seam and 48(48:52) sts down left front neck, **1st size only** k1, kfb, C3FP, [p2tog] twice, k2, p2, [k2tog] twice, p2, k2, [p2tog] twice, C3BP, C3FP, [p2tog] twice, k2, p2, [k2tog] twice, p2, k2, [p2tog] twice, C3BP, m1 pwise, k2, so reducing 56 sts on holder to 46 sts, **2nd and 3rd sizes only** [k2tog] twice, p2, k2, m1 pwise, p1, k2, p2, [k2tog] twice, p2, k2, m1 pwise, p1, k2, p2, [k2tog] twice, p2, k2, p1, m1 pwise, k2, p2, [k2tog] twice, p2, k2, p1, m1 pwise, k2, p2, [k2tog] twice, so reducing 56 sts on holder to 50 sts, pick up and k48(48:52) sts up right front neck. 220(224:232) sts.
1st round [P2, k2] to end.
This round **forms** rib and is repeated.
Rib 9 more rounds.
Cast off purlwise.

TO MAKE UP

Join side and sleeve seams. Sew sleeves into armholes, easing to fit.

Ariel

MEASUREMENTS

One size.

MATERIALS

- Thirteen 50g balls of Debbie Bliss cashmerino aran in Camel 29.
- Pair 5mm (US 8) knitting needles.
- 4.50mm (US 7) crochet hook.
- Cable needle.

TENSION

24 sts and 27 rows to 10cm/4in square over blackberry st using 5mm (US 8) needles.

ABBREVIATIONS

C4B = slip next 2 sts onto cable needle and hold at back of work, k2, then k2 from cable needle.
C4F = slip next 2 sts onto cable needle and hold to front of work, k2, then k2 from cable needle.
Cr5R = slip next 2 sts onto cable needle and hold at back of work, k3, then p2 from cable needle.
Cr5L = slip next 3 sts onto cable needle and hold to front of work, p2, then k3 from cable needle.
C6F = slip next 3 sts onto cable needle and hold to front of work, k3, then k3 from cable needle.
kpk = work [k1, p1, k1] all into next st.
s2togkpo = slip next 2 sts as if to k2tog, k1, pass 2 slipped sts over.
dc/sc = double crochet in UK, single crochet in US.

Also see page 6.

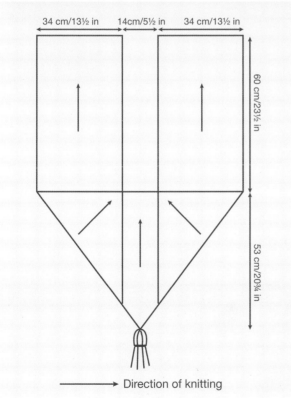

34 cm/13½ in   14cm/5½ in   34 cm/13½ in

60 cm/23½ in

53 cm/20¾ in

→ Direction of knitting

BACKS (make 2)

With 5mm (US 8) needles, cast on 165 sts.
Foundation row (right side) Purl.
1st row K1, p3tog, [kpk, p3tog] to last st, k1.
2nd row P1, ssk, p to last 3 sts, k2tog, p1.
The last 2 rows **form** the patt which decreases by 2 sts
|on every row, and are repeated.
Cont in patt until 5 sts rem, so ending with a right side row.
Next row K1, p3tog, k1.
Next row S2togkpo and fasten off.

LEFT FRONT

With right side facing and 5mm (US 8) needles, pick up
and k85 sts along left hand side edge of one back.
1st row (wrong side) K2, p4, k1, [kpk, p3tog] to last 6 sts,
k1, p4, k1.
2nd row P1, C4F, p to last 6 sts, C4B, p2.
3rd row K2, p4, k1, [p3tog, kpk] to last 6 sts, k1, p4, k1.
4th row P1, k4, p to last 6 sts, k4, p2.
These 4 rows **form** the patt and are repeated 35
times more.
Work first 3 rows of 36th repeat.
Next row (right side) Cast off, working k2tog over
centre 2 sts of each cable.

RIGHT FRONT

Work exactly as for Left Front, picking up 85 sts along
right hand side of other back.

CENTRE BACK PANEL

With 5mm (US 8) needles, cast on 4 sts.
1st row (right side) K4.
2nd row P1, m1, p2, m1, p1.
3rd row P1, m1, k4, m1, p1.
4th row K1, m1, p6, m1, k1.
5th row P1, m1, p1, C6F, p1, m1, p1.
6th row K1, m1, k2, p6, k2, m1, k1.
7th row K1, m1, p3, k6, p3, m1, k1.
8th row P1, m1, k4, p6, k4, m1, p1.
9th row K1, m1, k1, p4, k6, p4, k1, m1, k1.
10th row K1, m1, p2, k4, p6, k4, p2, m1, k1.
11th row K1, m1, k3, p4, C6F, p4, k3, m1, k1.
12th row P1, m1, k1, p3, k4, p6, k4, p3, k1, m1, p1.
13th row K1, m1, k1, p1, k3, p4, k6, p4, k3, p1, k1, m1, k1.
14th row P1, m1, p2, k1, p3, k4, p6, k4, p3, k1, p2, m1, p1.
15th row P1, m1, k3, p1, C5L, p2, k6, p2, C5R, p1, k3,
m1, p1.
16th row P1, m1, p4, k3, p3, k2, p6, k2, p3, k3, p4, m1, p1.
17th row K1, m1, p1, C4F, p3, C5L, C6F, C5R, p3, C4B,
p1, m1, k1.
18th row P1, m1, p1, k1, p4, k5, p12, k5, p4, k1, p1, m1, p1.

19th row K1, m1, k2, p1, k4, p5, [C6B] twice, p5, k4,
p1, k2, m1, k1.
20th row K1, m1, p3, k1, p4, k5, p12, k5, p4, k1, p3, m1, k1.
21st row P1, m1, C4B, p1, C4F, p3, C5R, C6F, C5L, p3,
C4B, p1, C4F, m1, p1. 44 sts.
** Now work in patt as follows:
1st row (wrong side) K2, p4, k1, p4, k3, p3, k2, p6, k2,
p3, k3, p4, k1, p4, k2.
2nd row P2, [k4, p1] twice, C5R, p2, k6, p2, C5L,
[p1, k4] twice, p2.
3rd and every foll wrong side row K all k sts and p all p sts.
4th row P2, C4B, p1, C4F, p1, k3, p4, k6, p4, k3, p1,
C4B, p1, C4F, p2.
6th row P2, [k4, p1] twice, k3, p4, C6F, p4, k3,
[p1, k4] twice, p2.
8th row As 4th row.
10th row P2, [k4, p1] twice, C5L, p2, k6, p2, C5R,
[p1, k4] twice, p2.
12th row P2, C4B, p1, C4F, p3, C5L, C6F, C5R, p3,
C4B, p1, C4F, p2.
14th row P2, k4, p1, k4, p5, [C6B] twice, p5, k4, p1, k4, p2.
16th row P2, C4B, p1, C4F, p3, C5R, C6F, C5L, p3, C4B,
p1, C4F, p2.
The last 16 rows **form** the patt and are repeated until the
straight edge of the panel fits along the edge of the Left
and Right Backs, ending with a 14th patt row.
Cast off, working [p1, p2tog, p1] across each 4-st cable
and [p1, p2tog, p2tog, p1] across each 6-st cable.

EDGING

Join centre back panel to left and right backs.
With **wrong** side facing, 4.50mm (US 7) crochet hook and
starting at lower edge of centre back, work [2dc/sc, miss 1]
all around edge of wrap working into edge st or row end.
Make a large tassle (approximately 15cm/6in long) and
stitch to lower point of centre back panel.

Odette

MEASUREMENTS

To fit bust

81–86	92–97	102–107	112–117	cm
32–34	36–38	40–42	44–46	in

FINISHED MEASUREMENTS

Bust

100	110	120	130	cm
39½	43¼	47¼	51¼	in

Width across back

48	53	58	62	cm
19	21	23	24½	in

Length to shoulder

72	74	76	78	cm
28¼	29¼	30	30¾	in

Sleeve length

46cm/18in for all sizes

MATERIALS

- 19(20:21:22) 50g balls of Debbie Bliss cashmerino dk in Teal 33.
- Pair each 3.75mm (US 5) and 4mm (US 6) knitting needles.
- Long 3.75mm (US 5) circular needle.
- Cable needle.

TENSION

26 sts and 32 rows to 10cm/4in square over patt using 4mm (US 6) needles.

ABBREVIATIONS

bind 3 = yarn to back of work, sl 1, k1, yf, k1, pass the slipped st over the k1, yf, k1.
C5FB = slip next 3 sts onto cable needle and hold to front of work, p2, then k3 from cable needle.
C5BP = slip next 2 sts onto cable needle and hold at back of work, k3, then p2 from cable needle.
C6B = slip next 3 sts onto cable needle and hold at back of work, k3, then k3 from cable needle.
C6F = slip next 3 sts onto cable needle and hold to front of work, k3, then k3 from cable needle.

Also see page 6.

Back & Fronts

72 (74: 76: 78) cm
28¼ (29¼: 30: 30¾) in

Sleeves

46 cm/18 in

49.5 (54.5: 59: 63.5) cm
19½ (21½: 23¼: 25) in

Odette

CABLE PANEL (worked over 44(44:54:54) sts)

1st row [P2, bind 3] 4(4:5:5) times, p4, [bind 3, p2] 4(4:5:5) times.
2nd row [K2, p3] 4(4:5:5) times, k4, [p3, k2] 4(4:5:5) times.
3rd to 6th rows Rep 1st and 2nd rows twice more.
7th row [P2, bind 3] 1(1:2:2) times, p2, [C5FB] 3 times, [C5BP] 3 times, p2, [bind 3, p2] 1(1:2:2) times.
8th row [K2, p3] 1(1:2:2) times, k4, [p3, k2] twice, p6, [k2, p3] twice, k4, [p3, k2] 1(1:2:2) times.
9th row [P2, bind 3] 1(1:2:2) times, p4, [C5FB] twice, C6B, [C5BP] twice, p4, [bind 3, p2] 1(1:2:2) times.
10th row [K2, p3] 1(1:2:2) times, k6, p3, k2, p12, k2, p3, k6, [p3, k2] 1(1:2:2) times.
11th row [P2, bind 3] 1(1:2:2) times, p6, C5FB, [C6F] twice, C5BP, p6, [bind 3, p2] 1(1:2:2) times.
12th row [K2, p3] 1(1:2:2) times, k8, p18, k8, [p3, k2] 1(1:2:2) times.
13th row [P2, bind 3] 1(1:2:2) times, p8, [C6B] 3 times, p8, [bind 3, p2] 1(1:2:2) times.
14th row As 12th row.
15th row [P2, bind 3] 1(1:2:2) times, p6, C5BP, [C6F] twice, C5FB, p6, [bind 3, p2] 1(1:2:2) times.
16th row As 10th row.
17th row [P2, bind 3] 1(1:2:2) times, p4, [C5BP] twice, C6B, [C5FB] twice, p4, [bind 3, p2] 1(1:2:2) times.
18th row As 8th row.
19th row [P2, bind 3] 1(1:2:2) times, p2, [C5BP] 3 times, [C5FB] 3 times, p2, [bind 3, p2] 1(1:2:2) times.
20th row As 2nd row.
21st to 24th rows Rep 1st and 2nd rows twice more.
These 24 rows **form** the patt and are repeated throughout.

BACK

With 4mm (US 6) needles cast on 129(141:153:165) sts.
1st row (right side) P1, [k1, p1] to end.
2nd row K to end.
These 2 rows **form** the patt and are repeated throughout.
Cont in patt until back measures 72(74:76:78)cm/
28¼(29¼:30:30¾)in from cast on edge, ending with a k row.
Shape shoulders
Cast off 15(16:18:20) sts at beg of next 4 rows and 14(16:18:18) sts at beg of foll 2 rows.
Cast off rem 41(45:45:49) sts.

POCKET LININGS (make 2)

With 4mm (US 6) needles cast on 28(28:36:36) sts.
1st row [P2, k2] 3(3:4:4) times, p4, [k2, p2] 3(3:4:4) times.
2nd row K to end.
These 2 rows **form** the patt and are repeated.
Work a further 49 rows.
Inc row (wrong side) [K2, p1, m1, p1] 3(3:4:4) times,

k4, [p1, m1, p1, k2] 3(3:4:4) times. 34(34:44:44) sts.
Leave these sts on a spare needle.

LEFT FRONT

With 4mm (US 6) needles, cast on 55(59:75:79) sts.
1st row (right side) K1, [p1, k1] 5(7:10:12) times, [p2, bind 3] 4(4:5:5) times, p4, [bind 3, p2] 4(4:5:5) times.
2nd row [K2, p3] 4(4:5:5) times, k4, [p3, k2] 3(3:4:4) times, p3, k13(17:23:27).
3rd to 10th rows Rep 1st and 2nd rows 4 times more.
11th row K1, [p1, k1] 5(7:10:12) times, work across 5th row of cable panel.
12th row Work across 6th row of cable panel, k11(15:21:25).
These 2 rows **set** the patt and are repeated throughout working correct patt panel rows.
Work a further 62 rows, so ending with 20th patt row.
Place pocket
Next row (right side) K1, [p1, k1] 5(7:10:12) times, p2, bind 3, place next 34(34:44:44) sts onto a holder, patt across 34(34:44:44) sts of first pocket lining, bind 3, p2.
Cont in patt until front measures 72(74:76:78)cm/
28¼(29¼:30:30¾)in from cast on edge, ending with a right side row.
Dec row [K2, p3] 1(1:2:2) times, [k2, p1, p2tog] 3 times, k4, [p1, p2tog, k2] 3 times, [p3, k2] 1(1:2:2) times, k11(15:21:25). 49(53:69:73) sts.
Shape shoulder
Cast off 17(19:23:25) sts at beg of next row and foll right side row.
Work 1 row.
Cast off rem 15(15:23:23) sts.

RIGHT FRONT

With 4mm (US 6) needles cast on 55(59:75:79) sts.
1st row (right side) [P2, bind 3] 4(4:5:5) times, p4, [bind 3, p2] 4(4:5:5) times, [k1, p1] 5(7:10:12) times, k1.
2nd row K13(17:23:27), p3, [k2, p3] 3(3:4:4) times, k4, [p3, k2] 4(4:5:5)times.
3rd to 10th rows Rep 1st and 2nd rows 4 times more.
11th row Work across 5th row of cable panel, [k1, p1] 5(7:10:12) times, k1.
12th row K11(15:21:25), work across 6th row of cable panel.
These 2 rows **set** the patt and are repeated throughout working correct patt panel rows.
Work a further 62 rows, ending patt row 20.
Place pocket
Next row (right side) P2, bind 3, place next 34(34:44:44) sts onto a holder, patt across 34(34:44:44) sts of pocket lining, bind 3, p2, [k1, p1] 5(7:10:12) times, k1.
Cont in patt until front measures 72(74:76:78)cm/

28¼(29¼:30:30¾)in from cast on edge, ending with a wrong side row.

Dec row [P2, bind 3] 1(1:2:2) times, [p2, k1, k2tog] 3 times, p4, [k1, k2tog, p2] 3 times, [bind 3, p2] 1 (1:2:2) times, [k1, p1] 5(7:10:12) times, k1.

Shape shoulder

Cast off 17(19:23:25) sts at beg of next and foll alt row.
Work 1 row.
Cast off rem 15(15:23:23) sts.

HOOD

Join shoulder seams.

On right and left fronts, place a marker on neck edge, 28(30:32:34) rows down from each shoulder.

With right side facing and 4mm (US 6) needles, pick up and k28(30:32:34) sts up right front from marker to shoulder, cast on 63(69:69:75) sts, pick up and k28(30:32:34) sts down left front to marker. 119(129:133:143) sts.

Next row (wrong side) K to end.

Beg with a 1st row, work in patt as given for Back.

Next 2 rows Patt to last 44 sts, turn.
Next 2 rows Patt to last 40 sts, turn.
Next 2 rows Patt to last 36 sts, turn.
Next 2 rows Patt to last 32 sts, turn.
Next 2 rows Patt to last 28 sts, turn.
Next 2 rows Patt to last 24 sts, turn.

Cont in this way working 4 more sts on each row until there are 4 sts left unworked at each side.

Next row Patt to end.

Cont in patt until hood measures 26(27:29:30)cm/10¼(10¾:11½:12)in from pick up row along front edge, ending with a 1st patt row.

Next row K58(63:65:70), k3tog, k to end.
Next row Patt to end.
Next row K57(62:64:69), k3tog, k to end.
Next row Patt to end.
Next row K56(61:63:68), k3tog, k to end.
Next row Patt to end.
Next row K55(60:62:67), k3tog, k to end.
Next row Patt to end.

Cont in this way and dec 2 sts at centre of row on next and 3 foll alt rows.
Cast off.

SLEEVES

With 4mm (US 6) needles, cast on 86(90:94:98) sts.

1st rib row (right side) K2, [p2, k2] to end.
2nd rib row P2, [k2, p2] to end.

Rep the last 2 rows for 10cm/4in ending with a 2nd rib row.

Cont in patt as follows:

1st row (right side) [K1, p1] to end.
2nd row K to end.

Work 6 rows.

Inc one st at each end of the next row and every foll 10th row until there are 102(106:110:114) sts.

Cont straight until sleeve measures 46cm/18in from cast on edge, ending with a right side row.
Cast off.

POCKET TOPS

With right side facing and 3.75mm (US 5) needles work across sts as follows:

1st row (right side) [P2, bind 3] 3(3:4:4) times, p4, [bind 3, p2] 3(3:4:4) times.
2nd row [K2, p3] 3(3:4:4) times, k4, [p3, k2] 3(3:4:4) times.

Rep the last 2 rows once more and the 1st row again.

Next row [K2, p1, p2tog] 3(3:4:4) times, k4, [p1 p2tog, k2] 3(3:4:4) times.

Cast off in patt.

RIGHT FRONT EDGING

With right side of right front facing, 3.75mm (US 5) circular needle and starting at lower edge, pick up and k214(222:230:238) sts from cast on edge to top of hood.

** **1st row** K2, [p1, yrn, p1, k2] to end. 267(277:287:297) sts.
2nd row P2, [bind 3, p2] to end.
3rd row K2, [p3, k2] to end.

Rep 2nd and 3rd rows 10(11:11:12) times more and the 2nd row again.

Next row K2, [p1, p2tog, k2] to end. 214(222:230:238) sts.

Cast off in rib.

LEFT FRONT EDGING

With right side of left front facing and 3.75mm (US 5) circular needle, pick up and k214(222:230:238) sts from top of hood to cast on edge.

Work exactly as Right Front Edging from ** to end.

TO MAKE UP

With centre of cast off edge of sleeve to shoulder, sew on sleeves. Join side and sleeve seams.

Join top hood and edging seam. Sew cast on edge of hood to cast off sts at back neck easing to fit. Sew down pocket tops and linings.

Jeanne

Length to shoulder

63	65	67	69	71	cm
24¾	25½	26½	27¼	28	in

Sleeve length

44	44	45	45	46	cm
17¼	17¼	17¾	17¾	18	in

MATERIALS

- 9(10:10:11:12) 50g balls of Debbie Bliss Luxury Tweed in Heather 17.
- Pair each of 4.50mm (US 7) and 5mm (US 8) knitting needles.
- 4.50mm (US 7) circular needle.
- 4 buttons.

TENSION

18 sts and 24 rows to 10cm/4in square over st st using 5mm (US 8) needles.

ABBREVIATIONS

See page 6.

BACK

With 5mm (US 8) needles cast on 90(94:102:106:114) sts.
1st row K2, [p2, k2] to end.
2nd row P2, [k2, p2] to end.
Rep the last 2 rows 9 times more and inc 2 sts evenly across last row on 2nd and 4th sizes only.
90(96:102:108:114) sts.
Beg with a k row, work in st st.
Work 14 rows.
Dec row K6, skpo, k to last 8 sts, k2tog, k6.
Work 3 rows.
Rep the last 4 rows 4 times more and the dec row again.
78(84:90:96:102) sts. **
Work 11(13:15:17:19) rows.
Inc row K3, m1, k to last 3 sts, m1, k3.
Work 5 rows.
Rep the last 6 rows 4 times more and the inc row again.
90(96:102:108:114) sts.
Work 7 rows.
Shape armholes
Cast off 7 sts at beg of next 2 rows. 76(82:88:94:100) sts.
Next row K2, skpo, k to last 4 sts, k2tog, k2.
Next row P to end.
Rep the last 2 rows 6(7:8:9:10) times more. 62(66:70:74:78) sts.
Cont in st st until armhole measures 20(21:22:23:24)cm/8(8¼:8¾:9:9½)in, ending with a p row.

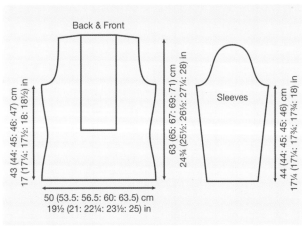

Back & Front

43 (44: 45: 46: 47) cm
17 (17¼: 17½: 18: 18½) in

63 (65: 67: 69: 71) cm
24¾ (25½: 26½: 27¼: 28) in

Sleeves

44 (44: 45: 45: 46) cm
17¼ (17¼: 17¾: 17¾: 18) in

50 (53.5: 56.5: 60: 63.5) cm
19½ (21: 22¼: 23½: 25) in

MEASUREMENTS

To fit bust

86	92	97	102	107	cm
34	36	38	40	42	in

FINISHED MEASUREMENTS

Bust

97	102	111	115	124	cm
38	40	43¾	45¼	48¾	in

Shape shoulders

Cast off 9(9:10:10:11) sts at beg of next 2 rows and 9(10:10:11:11) sts at beg of foll 2 rows.
Cast off rem 26(28:30:32:34) sts.

FRONT

Work as Back to **.
Work 9(11:13:15:17) rows.

Divide for front opening

Next row K26(28:30:32:34), turn and work on these sts |for first side of neck opening.
Next row P to end.
Inc row K3, m1, k to end.
Work 5 rows.
Rep the last 6 rows 4 times more and the inc row again. 32(34:36:38:40) sts.
Work 7 rows.

Shape armhole

Next row Cast off 7 sts, k to end. 25(27:29:31:33) sts.
Next row P to end.
Next row K2, skpo, k to end.
Next row P to end.
Rep the last 2 rows 6(7:8:9:10) times more. 18(19:20:21:22) sts.
Cont in st st until front measures same as Back to shoulder shaping, ending at armhole edge.

Shape shoulder

Next row Cast off 9(9:10:10:11) sts, k to end.
Next row P to end.
Cast off rem 9(10:10:11:11) sts.
With right side facing, rejoin yarn to rem sts, cast off centre 26(28:30:32:34) sts, k to end.
Next row P to end.
Inc row K to last 3 sts, m1, k3.
Work 5 rows.
Rep the last 6 rows 4 times more and the inc row again. 32(34:36:38:40) sts.
Work 8 rows.

Shape armhole

Next row Cast off 7 sts, p to end. 25(27:29:31:33) sts.
Next row K to last 4 sts, k2tog, k2.
Next row P to end.
Rep the last 2 rows 6(7:8:9:10) times more. 18(19:20:21:22) sts.
Cont in st st until front measures same as Back to shoulder shaping, ending at armhole edge.

Shape shoulder

Next row Cast off 9(9:10:10:11) sts, p to end.
Next row K to end.
Cast off rem 9(10:10:11:11) sts.

SLEEVES

With 5mm (US 8) needles, cast on 34(38:42:46:50) sts.
Work 16 rows in rib as given for Back.

Place a marker at each end of last row.
Change to 4.50mm (US 7) needles.
Rib a further 16 rows.
Change to 5mm (US 8) needles.
Beg with a k row, work in st st.
Work 2 rows.
Inc row K3, m1, k to last 3 sts, m1, k3.
Work 7 rows.
Rep the last 8 rows until there are 56(60:64:68:72) sts.
Cont straight until sleeve measures 44(44:45:45:46)cm/ 17¼(17¼:17¾:17¾:18)in from markers, ending with a p row.

Shape sleeve top

Cast off 7 sts st beg of next 2 rows. 42(46:50:54:58) sts.
Dec 1 st at each end of the next row and every foll 4th row until 24(28:32:36:40) sts rem, then on every foll right side row until 20(22:22:24:24) sts rem.
Work 1 row.
Cast off 3 sts at beg of next 2 rows.
Cast off rem 14(16:16:18:18) sts.

COLLAR

Join shoulder seams.
With 4.50mm (US 7) circular needle cast on one st, then pick up and k66(68:70:72:74) sts up left side of front neck, cast on 42(42:46:46:50) sts, pick up and k66(68:70:72:74) sts down left side of front neck, cast on one st. 176(180:188:192:200) sts.
1st row (wrong side) P3, [k2, p2] to last 5 sts, k2, p3.
2nd row K3, [p2, k2] to last 5 sts, p2, k3.
These 2 rows **form** the rib.
Rib a further 3 rows.
1st buttonhole row (right side) Rib 9, k2tog, y2rn, p2tog, rib 16, k2tog, y2rn, p2tog, rib to end.
2nd buttonhole row Rib to end working twice in y2rn.
Work a further 24(24:26:26:28) rows.
Rep the 2 buttonhole rows once again.
Rib a further 6 rows.
Cast off in rib.

TO MAKE UP

Lap right side of collar over left side and sew in place at centre front. Join side seams. Join sleeve seams. Sew sleeves into armholes easing to fit. Sew on buttons.

Estelle

MEASUREMENTS

To fit bust

86–91	97–102	107–112	cm
34–36	38–40	42–44	in

FINISHED MEASUREMENTS

Width across back

55	60	65	cm
21¾	23½	25½	in

Length (including lower edging)

78	79	81	cm
30¾	31	32	in

Sleeve

43	46	48	cm
17	18	19	in

MATERIALS

- 19(21:23) 50g balls of Debbie Bliss cashmerino aran in Silver 27.
- Pair each 4.50mm (US 7) and 5mm (US 8) knitting needles.
- Long 4.50mm (US 7) circular needle.
- Cable needle.

TENSION

22 sts and 26 rows to 10cm/4in square over cable patt using 5mm (US 8) needles.

ABBREVIATIONS

C4B = slip next 2 sts onto cable needle and hold at back of work, k2, then k2 from cable needle.
C4F = slip next 2 sts onto cable needle and hold to front of work, k2, then k2 from cable needle.

Also see page 6.

TIPS

- To cast on sts when shaping the front edges, just loop sts on with left thumb, for a firmer edge give the loop an extra turn before placing it on the needle.
- When picking up stitches along the straight edges of the fronts, miss approximately every 5th row-end.
- To make it easier to pick up the stitches neatly, do not join in new yarn at the front edges.

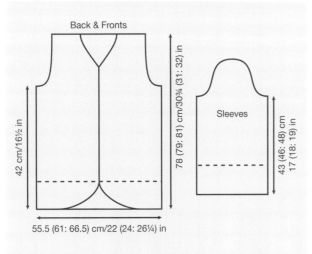

Back & Fronts

42 cm/16½ in

78 (79: 81) cm/30¾ (31: 32) in

Sleeves

43 (46: 48) cm
17 (18: 19) in

55.5 (61: 66.5) cm/22 (24: 26¼) in

BACK

With 5mm (US 8) needles, cast on 102(112:122) sts.
Foundation row (right side) K3, [* slip next st onto cable needle and hold at back of work, K2, then work kfb into st on cable needle, slip next 2 sts onto cable needle and hold at front of work, kfb, then k2 from cable needle *, k4] 9(10:11) times; rep from * to * once again, k3.
122(134:146) sts. This row is not repeated.
1st and every wrong side row P.
2nd row K.
4th row K1, [C4F, k4, C4B] 10(11:12) times, k1.
6th row K.
8th row K3, [C4B, C4F, k4] 9(10:11) times, C4B, C4F, k3.
1st to 8th rows **form** the patt and are repeated.
Work 101 more rows, so ending with 5th row of 14th patt from beg.
Shape armholes
Cast off 4 sts at beg of next 2 rows. 114(126:138) sts.
Dec row (right side) K1, k2tog, patt to last 3 sts, skpo, k1.
112(124:136) sts.
Cont in patt and dec in this way at each end of next 9 right side rows. 94(106:118) sts.
Patt 39(43:47) rows.
Cast off.

LEFT FRONT

With 5mm (US 8) needles, cast on 12 sts.
Foundation row (right side) K3, slip next st onto cable needle and hold at back of work, K2, then work kfb into st on cable needle, slip next 2 sts onto cable needle and hold to front of work, kfb, then k2 from cable needle, k3.
14 sts **.
1st and every wrong side row P.
2nd row K to end, do not turn, cast on 3 sts. 17 sts.
4th row K1, C4F, k4, C4B, C4F, cast on 3 sts. 20 sts.
6th row K to end, cast on 3 sts. 23 sts.
8th row K3, C4B, C4F, k4, C4B, C4F, cast on 3 sts. 26 sts.
The last 8 rows **set** cable patt to match Back.
Cont in patt and cast on 3 sts at end (front edge) of next 8(10:12) right side rows. 50(56:62) sts.
Patt 85(81:77) rows, so ending with a wrong side row.
Shape armhole
Cast off 4 sts at beg of next row. 46(52:58) sts.
P 1 row.
Dec row (right side) K1, k2tog, patt to end. 45(51:57) sts.
Cont in patt, dec in this way at beg of next 9 right side rows. 36(42:48) sts.
Patt 3 rows.
Shape neck
Dec row (right side) Patt to last 2 sts, skpo. 35(41:47) sts.
Cont in patt, dec in this way at end of next 11(13:13) right side rows. 24(28:34) sts.

Patt 13(13:17) rows.
Cast off.

RIGHT FRONT

Work as Left Front to **.
1st row P to end, do not turn, cast on 3 sts. 17 sts.
2nd row K.
3rd row As 1st row. 20 sts.
4th row K3, C4B, C4F, k4, C4B, k1.
The last row **sets** the cable patt to match Back.
Cont in patt and cast on 3 sts at end (front edge) of next 10(12:14) wrong side rows. 50(56:62) sts.
Patt 87(83:79) rows, so ending with a **right** side row.
Shape armhole
Cast off 4 sts at beg of next row. 46(52:58) sts.
Dec row (right side) Patt to last 3 sts, skpo, k1. 45(51:57) sts.
Cont in patt, dec in this way at end of next 9 right side rows. 36(42:48) sts.
Patt 3 rows.
Shape neck
Dec row (right side) K2tog, patt to end. 35(41:47) sts.
Cont in patt, dec in this way at beg of next 11(13:13) right side rows. 24(28:34) sts.
Patt 13(13:17) rows.
Cast off.

SLEEVES

With 5mm (US 8) needles, cast on 62(72:82) sts.
Foundation row (right side) K3, [* slip next st onto cable needle and hold at back of work, K2, then work kfb into st on cable needle, slip next 2 sts onto cable needle and hold at front of work, kfb, then k2 from cable needle *, k4] 5(6:7) times, rep from * to * once more, k3. 74(86:98) sts.
Cont in patt as given for Back, work 77(85:93) rows.
Shape top
Cast off 4 sts at beg of next 2 rows. 66(78:90) sts.
Dec row (right side) K1, k2tog, patt to last 3 sts, skpo, k1. 64(76:88) sts.
Cont in patt, dec in this way at each end of next 13 right side rows. 38(50:62) sts.
Patt 7(3:3) rows.
Next row Slipping first st, cast off 2 sts, patt to last 2 sts, skpo. 35(47:59) sts.
Next row Slipping first st, cast off 2 sts, p to last 2 sts, p2tog. 32(44:56) sts.
Work last 2 rows 3(4:5) more times. 14(20:26) sts.
Cast off.

CUFF

With right side facing and 4.50mm (US 7) needles, pick up and k62(72:82) sts along cast on edge of sleeve.

1st row (wrong side) P3, [k6, p4] 5(6:7) times, k6, p3.
2nd row [K2, skpo, p4, k2tog] 6(7:8) times, k2. 50(58:66) sts.
3rd row P3, [k4, p4] 5(6:7) times, k4, p3.
4th row K3, [p4, k4] 5(6:7) times, p4, k3.
3rd and 4th rows **only** form the rib and are repeated.
Rib 33 more rows, so ending with a right side row.
Cast off in rib.

COLLAR AND EDGING

Join shoulder seams. Join side seams.
Collar Place a marker at each side of centre 44 sts of back
neck edge.
With right side facing and 4.50mm (US 7) circular needle,
pick up and k 44 sts between markers.
1st row (wrong side) K4, [p4, k4] 5 times, pick up
and p4 sts, turn. 48 sts.
2nd row [K4, p4] 6 times, pick up and k 4 sts, turn. 52 sts.
3rd row P4, [k4, p4] 6 times, pick up and k 4 sts. 56 sts.
4th row [P4, k4] 7 times, pick up and p 4 sts, turn. 60 sts.
5th row K4, [p4, k4] 7 times, pick up and p 4 sts, turn. 64 sts.
6th row [K4, p4] 8 times, pick up and k 4 sts, turn. 68 sts.
7th row P4, [k4, p4] 8 times, pick up and k 4 sts, turn. 72 sts.
8th row [P4, k4] 9 times, pick up and p 4 sts, turn. 76 sts.
9th row K4, [p4, k4] 9 times, pick up and p 4 sts, turn. 80 sts.
10th row [K4, p4] 10 times, pick up and k 4 sts, turn. 84 sts.
Cont in rib as set picking up 4 sts knitwise or purlwise at
end of each row, work 11(13:15) more rows. 128(136:144) sts.
Edging
1st round [K4, p4] 16(17:18) times, pick up and
k 136(146:156) sts down straight edge and around
curved edge of left front, 120(132:144) sts across back,
136(146:156) sts around curved edge and up straight
edge of right front. 520(560:600) sts.
2nd round [K4, p4] to end.
The 2nd round **forms** the rib and is repeated.
Rib 35 more rounds, then cont the last round in rib until
level with lower edge left side seam.
Cast off loosely in rib.

TO MAKE UP

Sew sleeves into armholes, easing to fit. Join sleeve seams.

Adele

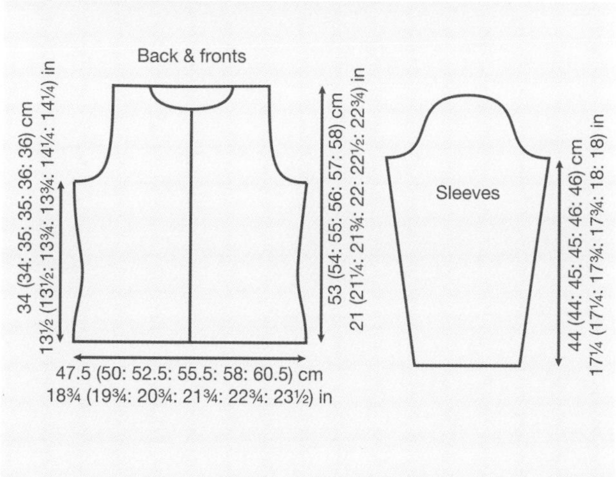

MEASUREMENTS

To fit bust

86	92	97	102	107	112	cm
34	36	38	40	42	44	in

FINISHED MEASUREMENTS

Bust

92	97	102	107	112	117	cm
36	38	40	42	44	46	in

Length to shoulder

53	54	55	56	57	58	cm
21	21¼	21¾	22	22½	22¾	in

Sleeve length

44	44	45	45	46	46	cm
17¼	17¼	17¾	17¾	18	18	in

MATERIALS

- 12(13:14:14:15:16) 50g balls Debbie Bliss Luxury Tweed in Burgundy 16.
- Pair each 4.50mm (US 7) and 5mm (US 8) knitting needles.
- 6 buttons.

TENSION

15 sts and 26 rows to 10cm/4in square over patt using 5mm (US 8) needles.

ABBREVIATIONS

See page 6.

Back & fronts

34 (34: 35: 35: 36: 36) cm
13½ (13½: 13¾: 13¾: 14¼: 14¼) in

53 (54: 55: 56: 57: 58) cm
21 (21¼: 21¾: 22: 22½: 22¾) in

47.5 (50: 52.5: 55.5: 58: 60.5) cm
18¾ (19¾: 20¾: 21¾: 22¾: 23½) in

Sleeves

44 (44: 45: 45: 46: 46) cm
17¼ (17¼: 17¾: 17¾: 18: 18) in

BACK

With 5mm (US 8) needles cast on 71(75:79:83:87:91) sts.
1st row (right side) K into front and back of each st to end.
2nd row K2tog, [p2tog, k2tog] to end.
3rd row K into front and back of each st to end.
4th row P2tog, [k2tog, p2tog] to end.
These 4 rows **form** the patt and are repeated throughout.
Cont straight until back measures 12(12:13:13:14:14)cm/
4¾(4¾:5:5:5½:5½)in from cast on edge, ending with
a wrong side row.
Change to 4.50mm (US 7) needles.
Work a further 6cm/2¼in in patt.
Change to 5mm (US 8) needles.
Cont straight until back measures 34(34:35:35:36:36)cm/
13½(13½:13¾:13¾:14¼:14¼)in from cast on edge, ending
with a wrong side row.
Shape armholes
Next row Cast off 6 sts, patt to last 7 sts, k7.
Next row Cast off 6 sts, patt to last st, k1.
Next row K1, work 2 tog, patt to last 3 sts, work 2 tog, k1.
Next row K2, patt to last 2 sts, k2.
Rep the last 2 rows 6 times more. 45(49:53:57:61:65) sts.
Cont straight until back measures
53(54:55:56:57:58)cm/21(21¼:21¾:22:22½:22¾)in from
cast on edge, ending with a wrong side row.
Shape shoulders
Next row Cast off 10(11:13:14:16:17) sts, patt to last
11(12:14:15:17:18) sts, k11(12:14:15:17:18).
Next row Cast off 10(11:13:14:16:17) sts, patt to last st, k1.
Cast off rem 25(27:27:29:29:31) sts.

LEFT FRONT

With 5mm (US 8) needles, cast on 39(41:43:45:47:49) sts.
1st row (right side) K into front and back of each st to end.
2nd row K2tog, [p2tog, k2tog] to end.
3rd row K into front and back of each st to end.
4th row P2tog, [k2tog, p2tog] to end.
These 4 rows **form** the patt and are repeated throughout.
Cont straight until front measures 12(12:13:13:14:14)cm/
4¾(4¾:5:5:5½:5½)in from cast on edge, ending with
a wrong side row.
Change to 4.50mm (US 7) needles.
Work a further 6cm/2¼in in patt.
Change to 5mm (US 8) needles.
Cont straight until front measures 34(34:35:35:36:36)cm/
13½(13½:13¾:13¾:14¼:14¼)in from cast on edge, ending
with a wrong side row.
Shape armhole
Next row Cast off 6 sts, patt to end.
Next row Patt to last st, k1.

Next row K1, work 2 tog, patt to end.
Next row Patt to last 2 sts, k2.
Rep the last 2 rows 6 times more. 26(28:30:32:34:36) sts.
Cont straight until front measures 47(48:48:49:49:50)cm/
18½(19:19:19¼:19¼:19¾)in from cast on edge, ending
with a wrong side row.
Shape neck
Next row Patt to last 8(8:9:9:10:10) sts, turn and
leave these 8(8:9:9:10:10) sts on a holder for collar.
Next row Patt to end.
Next row Patt to last 3 sts, work 2 tog, k1.
Next row K2, patt to end.
Rep the last 2 rows until 10(11:13:14:16:17) sts rem.
Work straight until front matches Back to shoulder
shaping, ending at armhole edge.
Shape shoulder
Cast off.

RIGHT FRONT

Mark positions on Left Front for 5 buttons, the first
10(10:11:11:12:12)cm/4(4:4¼:4¼:4¾:4¾)in from cast on
edge, the fifth 2cm/¾in below neck shaping and rem
three spaced evenly between and buttonholes are
worked to match button positions as follows:
1st buttonhole row (right side) Patt 4, yrn, p2tog, patt to end.
2nd buttonhole row Patt to last 10 sts, p2, patt to end.
With 5mm (US 8) needles, cast on 39(41:43:45:47:49) sts.
1st row (right side) K into front and back of each st to end.
2nd row K2tog, [p2tog, k2tog] to end.
3rd row K into front and back of each st to end.
4th row P2tog, [k2tog, p2tog] to end.
These 4 rows **form** the patt and are repeated throughout.
Cont straight until front measures 12(12:13:13:14:14)cm/
4¾(4¾:5:5:5½:5½)in from cast on edge, ending with
a wrong side row.
Change to 4.50mm (US 7) needles.
Work a further 6cm/2¼in in patt.
Change to 5mm (US 8) needles.
Cont straight until front measures 34(34:35:35:36:36)cm/
13½(13½:13¾:13¾:14¼:14¼)in from cast on edge, ending
with the same wrong side row as Left Front for armhole.
Next row Patt to last 7 sts, k7.
Shape armhole
Next row (wrong side) Cast off 6 sts, patt to end.
Next row Patt to last 3 sts, work 2 tog, k1.
Next row K2, patt to end.
Rep the last 2 rows 6 times more. 26(28:30:32:34:36) sts.
Cont straight until front measures 47(48:48:49:49:50)cm/
18½(19:19:19¼:19¼:19 ¾)in from cast on edge, ending
with a wrong side row.

Shape neck

Next row (right side) Patt 8(8:9:9:10:10) sts, and leave these 16(16:18:18:20:20)sts on a holder for collar, patt to end.
Next row Patt to end.
Next row K1, work 2 tog, patt to end.
Next row Patt to last 2 sts, k2.
Rep the last 2 rows until 10(11:13:14:16:17) sts rem.
Work straight until front matches Back to shoulder shaping, ending at armhole edge.

Shape shoulder

Cast off.

SLEEVES

With 5mm (US 8) needles, cast on 29(31:33:35:37:39) sts.
1st row (right side) K into front and back of each st to end.
2nd row K2tog, [p2tog, k2tog] to end.
3rd row K into front and back of each st to end.
4th row P2tog, [k2tog, p2tog] to end.
These 4 rows **form** the patt and are repeated throughout.
Work a further 12 rows.
Inc and work into patt one st at each end of the 3rd and every foll 6th row until there are 51(53:55:57:59:61) sts.
Cont straight until sleeve measures 44(44:45:45:46:46)cm/17¼(17¼:17¾:17¾:18:18)in from cast on edge, ending with a wrong side row.

Shape sleeve top

Next row Cast off 6 sts, patt to last 7 sts k7.
Next row Cast off 6 sts, patt to last st, k1.
Next row K1, work 2 tog, patt to last 3 sts, work 2 tog, k1.
Next row K2, patt to last 2 sts, k2.
Next row K2, patt to last 2 sts, k2.
Next row K2, patt to last 2 sts, k2.
Rep the last 4 rows 6 times more. 25(27:29:31:33:35) sts.
Next row K1, work 2 tog, patt to last 3 sts, work 2 tog, k1.
Next row K2, patt to last 2 sts, k2.
Rep the last 2 rows 3(3:4:4:5:5) times more.
17(19:19:21:21:23) sts.
Cast off.

COLLAR

Join shoulder seams.
With right side facing and 4.50mm (US 7) needles, slip 16(16:18:18:20:20) sts from right front neck holder onto a needle, pick up and k12(12:13:13:14:14) sts up right front neck, 25(27:27:29:29:31) sts from back neck, 12(12:13:13:14:14) sts down left front neck, then k into front and back of 8(8:9:9:10:10) sts from left front holder.
81(83:89:91:97:99) sts.

Next row (wrong side) [K2tog, p2tog] 4(4:4:4:5:5) times, k2tog 0(0:1:1:0:0) times, p49(51:53:55:57:59) sts, [k2tog, p2tog] 4(4:4:4:5:5) times, k2tog 0(0:1:1:0:0) times.
65(67:71:73:77:79) sts.
1st row (right side) K into front and back of each st to end.
2nd row K2tog, [p2tog, k2tog] to end.
3rd row K into front and back of each st to end.
4th row P2tog, [k2tog, p2tog] to end.
These 4 rows **form** the patt and are repeated throughout.
Patt a further 10 rows.
1st buttonhole row Patt 4, yrn, p2tog, patt to end.
2nd buttonhole row Patt to last 10 sts, p2, patt to end.
Patt a further 4 rows.
Next row K to end.
Change to 5mm (US 8) needles.
Beg with a 1st row, work 20 rows in patt.
Cast off.

TO MAKE UP

Join side and sleeve seams. Sew sleeves into armholes, easing to fit. Sew on buttons.

Elise

MATERIALS

- 20(22:25) 50g balls Debbie Bliss alpaca silk in Lilac 31.
- Pair 5mm (US 8) knitting needles.
- Cable needle.
- 4.50mm (US 7) crochet hook.

TENSION

18 sts and 24 rows to 10cm/4in square over reverse st st using 5mm (US 8) needles.

ABBREVIATIONS

C12F = slip next 6 sts onto cable needle and hold to front of work, k6, then k6 from cable needle.
C14F = slip next 7 sts onto cable needle and hold to front of work, k7, then k7 from cable needle.
dc/sc = double crochet in UK, single crochet in US.

Also see page 6.

NOTE

A single cable runs from the lower edge of the Right Front, up to the shoulder to meet the single cable on the Back. The front edge cable on the Right Front, transforms into a st st band along the front neck edge, extending around the back neck, this st st band is echoed on the Left Front. Each sleeve has either a central cable extending from the cuff or a central st st band echoing its corresponding front.

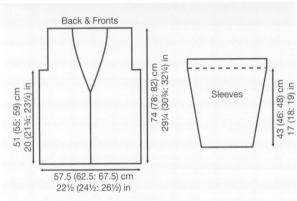

Back & Fronts

51 (55: 59) cm
20 (21¾: 23¼) in

74 (78: 82) cm
29¼ (30¾: 32¼) in

57.5 (62.5: 67.5) cm
22½ (24½: 26½) in

Sleeves

43 (46: 48) cm
17 (18: 19) in

MEASUREMENTS

To fit bust
81–86   92–97   102–107 cm
32–34   36–38   40–42in

FINISHED MEASUREMENTS

Bust
115   125   135cm
45¼   49¼   53¼in

Length to shoulder
74   78   82cm
29¼   30¾   32¼in

Sleeve length
43   46   48cm
17   18   19in

BACK

With 5mm (US 8) needles, cast on 111(120:129) sts.
1st row (right side) P10, k14, p to end.
2nd row K87(96:105), p14, k10.
3rd to 10th rows Rep 1st and 2nd rows 4 times more.
11th row P10, C14F, p to end.
12th, 13th and 14th rows As 2nd, 1st and 2nd rows.
These 14 rows **form** the patt and are repeated.
Cont in patt until back measures 51(55:59)cm/20(21¾:23¼)in from cast on edge, ending with a wrong side row.
Shape armholes
Keeping patt correct, cast off 9 sts at beg of next 2 rows.
93(102:111) sts.
Cont straight in patt as set until back measures 74(78:82)cm/29¼(30¾:32¼)in, ending with a wrong side row.
Shape shoulders
Next row (right side) Cast off 27(31:35) sts and dec 2 sts in centre of cable, p to end.
Next row Cast off 22(26:30) sts, k to end.
Cast off rem 44(45:46) sts.
Place a marker in centre of cast off edge.

LEFT FRONT

With 5mm (US 8) needles, cast on 58(63:68) sts.
1st row (right side) P45(50:55), k12, p1.
2nd row K1, p12, k45(50:55).
These 2 rows **form** the patt and are repeated.
Cont in patt until left front measures 38(40:42)cm/
15(15¾:16½)in from cast on edge, ending with
a wrong side row.
Shape front slope
Dec row (right side) P to last 15 sts, p2tog, k12, p1.
Keeping patt correct, dec 1 st at inner edge of st st front
band as before, on 12(13:14) foll 6th rows and **at the same
time**, when front measures 51(55:59)cm/20(21¾:23¾)in
from cast on edge, cast off 9 sts at beg of next right side
row for armhole.
When all decs have been worked, cont in patt as set on
rem 36(40:44) sts until left front measures same as Back
to shoulder, ending at armhole edge.
Shape shoulder and work neckband
Next row (right side) Cast off 22(26:30) sts, k next 12, p1.
Next row K1, p12, k1.
Cont in patt as set on rem 14 sts until neckband fits
across back neck edge to centre back marker.
Cast off.

RIGHT FRONT

With 5mm (US 8) needles, cast on 65(70:75) sts.
1st row (right side) P1, k14, p26(31:36), k14, p10.
2nd row K10, p14, k26(31:36), p14, k1.
3rd to 10th rows Rep 1st and 2nd rows 4 times more.
11th row P1, C14F, p26(31:36), C14F, p10.
12th, 13th and 14th rows As 2nd, 1st and 2nd rows.
These 14 rows **form** the patt and are repeated.
Cont in patt until right front measures 38(40:42)cm/
15(15¾:16½)in from cast on edge, ending with a wrong side row.
Shape front slope
Next row (right side) Patt 15, p2tog, patt to end.
Patt 5 rows.
Rep the last 6 rows until right front measures
51(55:59)cm/20(21¾:23¼)in from cast on edge, ending
with a right side row.
Shape armhole
Next row Cast off 9 sts, patt to end.
Keeping patt correct, cont to dec 1 st for front slope at
inner edge of cable on every 6th row as before and work
until the next 11th patt row has been worked, so ending
with a cable row.
Next row (wrong side) K1, p14, k to last 15 sts, p5,
[p2tog] twice, p5, k1.
Next row P1, k12, p to last 15 sts, k14, p1.
Next row K1, p14, k to last 13 sts, p12, k1.
Cont in patt as now set, working cable at armhole edge

only, front edge cable sts as st st and decreasing for front
slope at inner edge of st st as before until 41(45:49) sts
rem, then cont straight until right front measures same
as Back to shoulder, ending at armhole edge.
Shape shoulder and work neckband
Next row (wrong side) Cast off 27(31:35) sts, decreasing
2 sts in centre of cable, p next 12 sts, k1.
Cont in patt as set on rem 14 sts until collar fits across
back neck edge to centre back marker.
Cast off.

LEFT SLEEVE

With 5mm (US 8) needles, cast on 52 sts.
1st row (right side) P5, k12, [p3, k12] twice, p5.
2nd row K5, p12, [k3, p12] twice, k5.
Rep the last 2 rows 3 times more.
9th row P5, C12F, [p3, C12F] twice, p5.
10th row As 2nd row.
11th row As 1st row.
Rep the last 2 rows 4 times more then the 10th row again.
21st row As 9th row.
22nd row As 2nd row.
23rd row P20, k12, p20.
24th row K20, p12, k20.
Cont in patt as set by last 2 rows, so working a central
st st panel with reverse st st to either side, **at the same
time**, inc 1 st at each end of next and every foll 4th row
until there are 84(88:92) sts, taking all inc sts into reverse st st.
Cont straight until sleeve measures 43(46:48)cm/17(18:19)in
from cast on edge, mark each end of last row, then work
a further 12 rows.
Cast off in patt.

RIGHT SLEEVE

Work exactly as Left Sleeve but cont to work cable on
centre 12 sts only for the full length of the sleeve.

TO MAKE UP

Matching cable on right front to cable on back, join
shoulder seams. Matching centre of cast off edge of
sleeve to shoulder, sew sleeves into armholes with row
ends above markers sewn to sts cast off at underarm.
Join side and sleeve seams. Join cast off edges of
neckband, then sew row ends of neckband to back neck.

EDGING

With wrong side facing and 4.50mm (US 7) crochet hook,
starting at lower edge of left front, join on yarn and work
1dc/sc into every other edge st, up left front across
neckband and down right front. Fasten off.

Thandie

Back & Fronts

58 (59: 60: 61) cm
22¾ (23¼: 23½: 24) in

78 (80: 82: 84) cm
30¾ (31½: 32¼: 33) in

Sleeves

46 (46: 48: 48) cm
18 (18: 19: 19) in

52.5 (60: 67.5: 74.5) cm
20¾ (23½: 26½: 29¼) in

BACK

With 4.50mm (US 7) needles, cast on 100(114:128:142) sts.
1st row (wrong side) K to end.
2nd and 3rd rows P to end.
4th row K to end.
5th row P to end.
6th row (right side) K8, [MB, k6] to last 8 sts, MB, k7.
7th row P to end.
8th and 9th rows K to end.
10th and 11th rows P to end.
Rep 8th to 11th rows 19 times more, so ending with
a wrong side row.
Change to 5mm (US 8) needles.
1st row K3, [p3, k4] to last 6 sts, p3, k3.
2nd row P to end.
These 2 rows **form** the patt and are repeated throughout.
Cont in patt until back measures 58(59:60:61)cm/
22¾(23¼:23½:24)in from cast on edge, ending with
a wrong side row.
Shape armholes
Cast off 9 sts at beg of next 2 rows. 82(96:110:124) sts.
Cont straight until back measures 78(80:82:84)cm/
30¾(31½:32¼:33)in from cast on edge, ending with
a wrong side row.
Shape shoulders
Cast off 9(11:13:15) sts at beg of next 6 rows.
Cast off rem 28(30:32:34) sts.

POCKET LININGS (make 2)

With 4.50mm (US 7) needles, cast on 27(29:31:33) sts.
Beg with a k row, work in st st until pocket lining measures
15(16:16:17)cm/6(6¼:6¼:6¾)in from cast on edge, ending
with a k row.
Leave these sts on a holder.

LEFT FRONT

With 4.50mm (US 7) needles, cast on 55(62:69:76) sts.
1st row (wrong side) K to end.
2nd and 3rd rows P to end.
4th row K to end.
5th row K10, p to end.
6th row K8, [MB, k6] to last 12 sts, MB, k1, p10.
7th row P to end.
8th and 9th rows K to end.
10th and 11th rows P to end.
Rep 8th to 11th rows 18 times more then the 8th and 9th
rows only of 19th rep, so ending with a wrong side row.
Place pocket
Next row (right side) P9(12:15:18), cast off next
27(29:31:33) sts, p to end.
Next row P19(21:23:25), p across 27(29:31:33) sts

of pocket lining, p9(12:15:18).
Change to 5mm (US 8) needles.
1st row (right side) K3, [p3, k4] to last 17 sts, p3, k14.
2nd row K10, p to end.
3rd row K3, [p3, k4] to last 10 sts, p10.
4th row P to end.
These 4 rows **form** the patt and are repeated throughout.
Cont in patt until front measures 58(59:60:61)cm/
22¾(23¼:23½:24)in from cast on edge, ending with
a wrong side row.
Shape armhole
Next row Cast off 9 sts, patt to end. 46(53:60:67) sts.
Cont straight until front measures 72(73:75:76)cm/
28¼(28¾:29½:30)in from cast on edge, ending with
a right side row.
Shape neck
Next row Cast off 10 sts, patt to end. 36(43:50:57) sts.
Dec one st at neck edge on next 9(10:11:12) rows.
27(33:39:45) sts.
Work straight until front measures same as Back
to shoulder, ending at armhole edge.
Shape shoulder
Cast off 9(11:13:15) sts at beg of next row and foll alt row.
Work 1 row.
Cast off rem 9(11:13:15) sts.
Place markers for 7 buttons, the first level with first row
of pocket opening, the seventh 2cm/¾in below neck
shaping, with the rem 5 spaced evenly between.

RIGHT FRONT

With 4.50mm (US 7) needles cast on 55(62:69:76) sts.
1st row (wrong side) K to end.
2nd and 3rd rows P to end.
4th row K to end.
5th row P to last 10 sts, k10.
6th row P10, k2, [MB, k6] to last 8 sts, MB, k7.
7th row P to end.
8th and 9th rows K to end.
10th and 11th rows P to end.
Rep 8th to 11th rows 18 times more then the 8th and 9th
rows only of 19th rep, so ending with a wrong side row.
Place pocket
Next row (buttonhole row) P3, p2tog, y2rn, p2tog,
p12(14:16:18), cast off next 27(29:31:33) sts, p to end.
Next row P9(12:15:18), p across 27(29:31:33) sts of
pocket lining, p19(21:23:25).
Change to 5mm (US 8) needles.
1st row (right side) K14, [p3, k4] to last 6 sts, p3, k3.
2nd row P to last 10 sts, k10.
3rd row P10, k4, [p3, k4] to last 6 sts, p3, k3.
4th row P to end.
These 4 rows **form** the patt and are repeated throughout.

Working buttonholes as set to match markers, cont in patt until front measures 58(59:60:61)cm/22¾(23¼:23½:24)in from cast on edge, ending with a right side row.

Shape armhole

Next row Cast off 9 sts, patt to end. 46(53:60:67) sts.
Cont straight until front measures 72(73:75:76)cm/28¼(28¾:29½:30)in from cast on edge, ending with a wrong side row.

Shape neck

Next row Cast off 10 sts, patt to end. 36(43:50:57) sts.
Dec one st at neck edge on next 9(10:11:12) rows. 27(33:39:45) sts.
Work straight until front measures same as Back to shoulder, ending at armhole edge.

Shape shoulder

Cast off 9(11:13:15) sts at beg of next and foll alt row.
Work 1 row.
Cast off rem 9(11:13:15) sts.

SLEEVES

With 4.50mm (US 7) needles cast on 37(44:44:51) sts.
1st row (wrong side) K to end.
2nd and 3rd rows P to end.
4th row K to end.
5th row P to end.
6th row (right side) K1, [MB, k6] to last 8 sts, MB, k7.
7th row P to end.
8th and 9th rows K to end.
10th and 11th rows P to end.
Rep 8th to 11th rows 7 times more, so ending with a wrong side row.
Change to 5mm (US 8) needles.
1st row (right side) K3, [p3, k4] to last 6 sts, p3, k3.
2nd row P to end.
These 2 rows **set** the patt and are repeated throughout.
Keeping patt correct, inc 1 st at each end of the next row and every foll 6th row until there are 45(52:52:59) sts, then on every foll 4th row until there are 75(82:84:89) sts, taking all inc sts into patt.
Work straight until sleeve measures 46(46:48:48)cm/18(18:19:19)in from cast on edge, ending with a wrong side row.
Place markers at each end of last row.
Work a further 12 rows straight.
Cast off.

COLLAR

Join shoulder seams.
With 4.50mm (US 7) needles, miss first 5 sts cast off on right front, pick up and k5 sts along rem 5 sts, 20(22:24:26) sts up right front to shoulder, 28(30:32:34) sts from back neck, 20(22:24:26) sts down left front, then

5 sts from first 5 sts on left front band. 78(84:90:96) sts.
Beg with a k row, work in st st.
Next 2 rows Work to last 5 sts, turn.
Next 2 rows Work to last 10 sts, turn.
Next 2 rows Work to last 15 sts, turn.
Next 2 rows Work to last 20 sts, turn.
Next 2 rows Work to last 25 sts, turn.
Next row K to end.
Change to 5mm (US 8) needles and work in patt as follows:
1st row (wrong side of collar, right side of jacket) K to end.
2nd and 3rd rows P to end.
4th row K to end.
5th row K to end.
Rep 2nd to 5th rows 5 times more then the 2nd and 3rd patt rows once again.
Next row K6, [MB, k5] to last 6 sts, MB, k5.
Next row K5, p to last 5 sts, k5.
K 2 rows
Next row K5, p to last 5 sts, k5.
Cast off.

TO MAKE UP

Sew sleeves into armholes easing to fit, and with row ends above markers sewn to sts cast off at underarm. Join side and sleeve seams. Sew on buttons.

Natalie

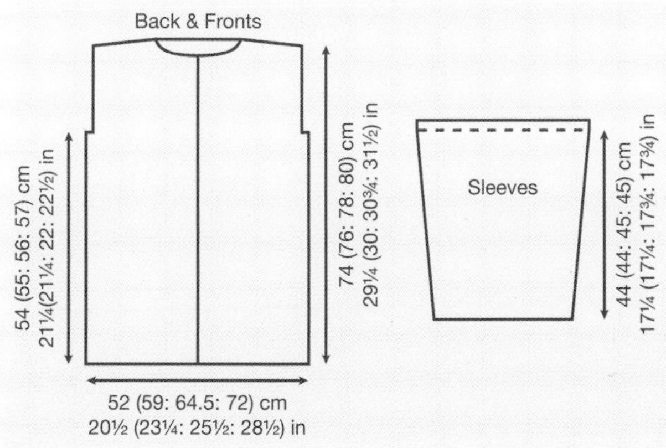

MEASUREMENTS

To fit bust

81–86	92–97	102–107	112–117	cm
32–34	36–38	40–42	44–46	in

FINISHED MEASUREMENTS

Bust

102	116	128	142	cm
40	45½	50½	56	in

Width across back

52	58	64	71	cm
20½	22¾	25½	28	in

Length to shoulder

74	76	78	80	cm
29¼	30	30¾	31½	in

Sleeve length

44	44	45	45	cm
17¼	17¼	17¾	17¾	in

MATERIALS

- 18(19:21:22) 50g balls of Debbie Bliss cashmerino dk in Forest 31.
- Pair each 3.75mm (US 5) and 4mm (US 6) knitting needles.
- Circular 3.75mm (US 5) and 4mm (US 6) knitting needles.

TENSIONS

22 sts and 30 rows over patt and 28 sts and 30 rows to rib when slightly stretched, both to 10cm/4in square using 4mm (US 6) needles.

ABBREVIATIONS

See page 6.

BACK

With 3.75mm (US 5) needles, cast on 114(130:142:158) sts.
1st rib row (right side) K2, [p2, k2] to end.
2nd rib row P2, [k2, p2] to end.
Rep the last 2 rows until work measures 20cm/8in from cast on edge, ending with a 2nd row.
Change to 4mm (US 6) needles and work in patt as follows:
1st row (right side) K to end.
2nd row P2, [k2, p2] to end.
These 2 rows **form** the patt and are repeated.

Back & Fronts

54 (55: 56: 57) cm
21¼(21¼: 22: 22½) in

74 (76: 78: 80) cm
29¼ (30: 30¾: 31½) in

52 (59: 64.5: 72) cm
20½ (23¼: 25½: 28½) in

Sleeves

44 (44: 45: 45) cm
17¼ (17¼: 17¾: 17¾) in

Cont straight until back measures 54(55:56:57)cm/ 21¼(21¾:22:22½)in from cast on edge, ending with a wrong side row.

Shape armholes

Cast off 7(11:11:15) sts at beg of next 2 rows. 100(108:120:128) sts.

Cont in patt until back measures 74(76:78:80)cm/ 29¼(30:30¾:31½)in from cast on edge, ending with a wrong side row.

Shape shoulders

Cast off 9(10:11:12) sts at beg of next 4 rows and 9(9:11:11) sts at beg of foll 2 rows.
Cast off rem 46(50:54:58) sts.

LEFT FRONT

With 3.75mm (US 5) needles, cast on 92(100:108:120) sts.
1st rib row (right side) K2, [p2, k2] to last 6 sts, p2, k4.
2nd rib row [K2, p2] to end.
Rep the last 2 rows until work measures 20cm/8in from cast on edge, ending with a 2nd row.
Cont in patt with rib border as follows:
1st row (right side) With 4mm (US 6) needle, k60(68:76:88), with 3.75mm (US 5) needle, [k2, p2] 7 times, k4.
2nd row With 3.75mm (US 5) needle, [k2, p2] 8 times, with 4mm (US 6) needle, [k2, p2] 15(17:19:22) times.
These 2 rows **form** the patt and are repeated.
Cont straight until front measures 54(55:56:57)cm/ 21¼(21¾:22:22½)in from cast on edge, ending with a wrong side row.

Shape armhole

Next row Cast off 7(11:11:15) sts, patt to end. 85(89:97:105) sts.
Cont in patt until 8 rows less have been worked than Back to shoulder shaping, ending with a wrong side row.

Shape neck

Next row Patt 53(57:65:73), turn and work on these sts only, leave rem 32 sts on a holder.
Next row (wrong side) Cast off 6(8:12:18) sts, patt to end.
Next row Patt to end.
Next row Cast off 6 sts, patt to end.
Next row Patt to end.
Next row Cast off 5 sts, patt to end.
Next row Patt to end.
Next row Cast off 4 sts, patt to end.

Shape shoulder and neck

Next row (right side) Cast off 9(10:11:12) sts, patt to end.
Next row Cast off 3 sts, patt to end.
Next row Cast off 9(10:11:12) sts, patt to end.
Next row Cast off 2 sts, patt to end.
Cast off rem 9(9:11:11) sts.

RIGHT FRONT

With 3.75mm (US 5) needles cast on 92(100:108:120) sts.
1st rib row (right side) K4, [p2, k2] to end.
2nd rib row [P2, k2] to end.
Rep the last 2 rows until work measures 20cm/8in from cast on edge, ending with a 2nd row.
Cont in patt with rib border as follows:
1st row (right side) With 3.75mm (US 5) needle, k4, [p2, k2] 7 times, with 4mm (US 6) needle, k60(68:76:88).
2nd row With 4mm (US 6) needle, [p2, k2] 15(17:19:22) times, with 3.75mm (US 5) needle, [p2, k2] 8 times.
These 2 rows **form** the patt and are repeated.
Cont straight until front measures 54(55:56:57)cm/ 21¼(21¾:22:22½)in from cast on edge, ending with a right side row.

Shape armhole

Next row (wrong side) Cast off 7(11:11:15) sts, patt to end. 85(89:97:105) sts.
Cont in patt, until 7 rows less have been worked than Back to shoulder shaping, so ending with a right side row.

Shape neck

Next row Patt 53(57:65:73), turn and work on these sts only, leave rem 32 sts on a holder.
Next row (right side) Cast off 6(8:12:18) sts, patt to end.
Next row Patt to end.
Next row Cast off 6 sts, patt to end.
Next row Patt to end.
Next row Cast off 5 sts, patt to end.
Next row Patt to end.
Next row Cast off 4 sts, patt to end.

Shape shoulder and neck

Next row (wrong side) Cast off 9(10:11:12) sts, patt to end.
Next row Cast off 3 sts, patt to end.
Next row Cast off 9(10:11:12) sts, patt to end.
Next row Cast off 2 sts, patt to end.
Cast off rem 9(9:11:11) sts.

SLEEVES

With 3.75mm (US 5) needles cast on 74(78:86:90) sts.
1st rib row (right side) K2, [p2, k2] to end.
2nd rib row P2, [k2, p2] to end.
Rep the last 2 rows until work measures 12cm/4¾in from cast on edge, ending with a 2nd row.
Change to 4mm (US 6) needles and work in patt as follows:
1st row (right side) K to end.
2nd row P2, [k2, p2] to end.
These 2 rows **form** the patt and are repeated.
Cont in patt and inc one st at each end of the 3rd and every foll 10th row until there are 92(96:102:106) sts, taking inc sts into patt.

Cont straight until sleeve measures 44(44:45:45)cm/
17¼(17¼:17¾:17¾)in from cast on edge, ending with
a wrong side row.
Place markers at each end of last row.
Work a further 6(8:8:10) rows.
Cast off.

COLLAR

Join shoulder seams.
With right side facing and 3.75mm (US 5) circular needle,
slip 32 sts from right front neck holder onto needle,
pick up and k32(34:38:44) sts up right front neck,
cast on 58(62:66:70) sts, pick up and k32(34:38:44) sts
down left front neck, then rib 32 sts from left front holder.
186(194:206:222) sts.
1st rib row (wrong side) K2, [p2, k2] to end.
2nd rib row K4, [p2, k2] to last 6 sts, p2, k4.
Rep the last 2 rows for 8cm/3in.
Change to 4mm (US 6) circular needle.
Cont in rib for a further 8cm/3in.
Cast off loosely but evenly in rib.

TO MAKE UP

Sew sleeves into armholes easing to fit and with row ends
above markers sewn to sts cast off at underarm.
Join side and sleeve seams.

Charlotte

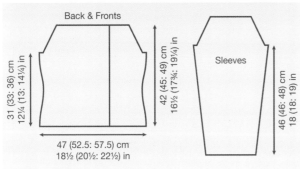

Back & Fronts

Sleeves

31 (33: 36) cm
12¼ (13: 14¼) in

42 (45: 49) cm
16½ (17¾: 19¼) in

47 (52.5: 57.5) cm
18½ (20½: 22½) in

46 (46: 48) cm
18 (18: 19) in

MEASUREMENTS

To fit bust

81–86	92–97	102–107	cm
32–34	36–38	40–42	in

FINISHED MEASUREMENTS

Bust

94	104	114	cm
37	41	45	in

Length to collar

42	45	49	cm
16½	17¾	19¼	in

Sleeve length

46	46	48	cm
18	18	19	in

MATERIALS

- 11(12:13) 50g balls of Debbie Bliss cashmerino dk in Damson 32.
- Pair size 4mm (US 6) knitting needles.
- 3¾mm (US 5) and 4mm (US 6) circular needles.
- 9(11:10) buttons.

TENSION

22 sts and 30 rows to 10cm/4in square over st st using 4mm (US 6) needles.

ABBREVIATIONS

See page 6.

BACK

With 4mm (US 6) needles, cast on 103(115:127) sts.
Moss st row (right side) K1, [p1, k1] to end.
Rep the last row 7 times more.
Beg with a k row, work in 6 rows in st st, so ending with a p row.
Dec row K3, ssk, k to last 5 sts, k2tog, k3.
Work 5 rows in st st.
Rep the last 6 rows 4 times more, then the dec row again.
91(103:115) sts.
Work 7(9:13) rows in st st.
Inc row K3, m1, k to last 3 sts, m1, k3.
Work 5 rows in st st.
Rep the last 6 rows 4 times more then the inc row once more. 103(115:127) sts.
Work 9(13:19) rows, so ending with a p row.
Shape underarm and raglans
Cast off 5(6:7) sts at beg of next 2 rows. 93(103:113) sts.
Next row K2, ssk, k to last 4 sts, k2tog, k2.
P 1 row.
Rep the last 2 rows 4(5:6) times more. 83(91:99) sts.
Work 2 rows.
Next row K2, ssk, k to last 4 sts, k2tog, k2.
Work 1 row.
Rep the last 4 rows 5 times more. 71(79:87) sts.
Leave these sts on a holder.

LEFT FRONT

With 4mm (US 6) needles, cast on 43(47:51) sts.
Moss st row P1, [k1, p1] to end.
Rep the last row 7 times more.
Next row (right side) K 38(42:46), moss st 5.
Next row Moss st 5, p to end.
These 2 rows **form** st st with moss st front edge.
Rep the last 2 rows twice more.
Dec row K3, ssk, k to last 5 sts, moss st 5.

Patt 5 rows.
Rep the last 6 rows 4 times more, then the dec row again.
37(41:45) sts.
Patt 7(9:13) rows.
Inc row K3, m1, k to last 5 sts, moss st 5.
Patt 5 rows.
Rep the last 6 rows 4 times more then the inc row
once more. 43(47:51) sts.
Work 9(13:19) rows, so ending with a wrong side row.
Shape underarm and raglan
Cast off 5(6:7) sts at beg of next row. 38(41:44) sts.
Patt 1 row.
Dec row K2, ssk, k to last 5 sts, moss st 5.
Patt 1 row.
Rep the last 2 rows 4(5:6) times more. 33(35:37) sts.
Patt 2 rows.
Dec row K2, ssk, k to last 5 sts, moss st 5.
Patt 1 row.
Rep the last 4 rows 5 times more. 27(29:31) sts.
Leave these sts on a holder.

RIGHT FRONT

With 4mm (US 6) needles, cast on 69(75:81) sts.
Work 4 rows in moss st as given for Left Front.
1st buttonhole row (right side) P1, k1, yf, k2tog, p1,
[k1, p1] to end.
Work a further 6(8:7) buttonholes in the moss st front edge
as before with 19(15:19) rows between and work patt and
shaping as follows:
Moss st 3 more rows.
Next row P1, [k1, p1] twice, k to end.
Next row P to last 4 sts, [k1, p1] twice.
The last 2 rows **form** st st with moss st front edge and
are repeated twice more, so ending with a wrong side row.
Next row (dec row) Moss st 5, k to last 5 sts, k2tog, k3.
Patt 5 rows.
Rep the last 6 rows 4 times more, then the dec row again.
63(69:75) sts.
Patt 7(9:13) rows.
Inc row Moss st 5, k to last 3 sts, m1, k3.
Patt 5 rows.
Rep the last 6 rows 4 times more then the inc row
once more. 69(75:81) sts.
Work 10(14:20) rows, so ending with a **right** side row.
Shape underarm and raglan
Cast off 5(6:7) sts at beg of next row. 64(69:74) sts.
Dec row Moss st 5, k to last 4 sts, k2tog, k2.
Patt 1 row.
Rep the last 2 rows 4(5:6) times more. 59(63:67) sts.
Patt 2 rows.
Dec row Moss st 5, k to last 4 sts, k2tog, k2.
Patt 1 row.
Rep the last 4 rows 5 times more. 53(57:61) sts.
Leave these sts on a holder.

SLEEVES

With 4mm (US 6) needles, cast on 49(51:53) sts.
Work 8 rows in moss st as given for Back.
Beg with a k row, work in 8 rows in st st, so ending
with a p row.
Inc row K2, m1, k to last 2 sts, m1, k2.
Work 7 rows.
Rep the last 8 rows until there are 75(81:87) sts.
Cont straight until sleeve measures 46(46:48)cm/18(18:19)in
from cast on edge, ending with a p row.
Shape underarm and raglan
Cast off 5(6:7) sts at beg of next 2 rows. 65(69:73) sts.
Next row K2, ssk, k to last 4 sts, k2tog, k2.
P 1 row.
Rep the last 2 rows 4(5:6) times more. 55(57:59) sts.
Work 2 rows.
Next row K2, ssk, k to last 4 sts, k2tog, k2.
Work 1 row.
Rep the last 4 rows 5 times more. 43(45:47) sts.
Leave these sts on a holder.

COLLAR

Join raglan seams.
With right side facing and 3¾mm (US 5) circular needle,
patt across first 52(56:60) sts of right front, k last st tog with
first st of right sleeve, k across 41(43:45) sts of right sleeve,
k last st tog with first st of back, k across 69(77:85) sts of
Back, k last st tog with first st of left sleeve, k across
41(43:45) sts of left sleeve, k last st tog with first st of left
front, then patt across rem 26(28:30) sts of left front.
233(251:269) sts.
1st row (wrong side) P1, [k1, p1] to end.
2nd row [P1, k1] twice, p2, [k1, p1] to last 5 sts,
[p1, k1] twice, p1.
These 2 rows **form** the single rib with moss st front
edges and are repeated.
Work 13 rows in patt.
Buttonhole row (right side) P1, k1, yf, k2tog, p2,
[k1, p1] to last 5 sts, p1, [k1, p1] twice.
Patt 2 rows.
Change to 4mm (US 6) circular needle and patt
a further 17 rows.
Work the buttonhole row again.
Cont in patt for a further 7cm/2¾in.
Cast off in patt.

TO MAKE UP

Join side and sleeve seams. Sew on buttons.

Distributors

For stockists of Debbie Bliss yarns
please contact:

UK & WORLDWIDE DISTRIBUTORS

Designer Yarns Ltd

Units 8–10 Newbridge Industrial Estate
Pitt Street, Keighley
W. Yorkshire BD21 4PQ
UNITED KINGDOM

T: +44 (0)1535 664222
F: +44 (0)1535 664333
E: alex@designeryarns.uk.com
www.designeryarns.uk.com

USA

Knitting Fever Inc.

315 Bayview Avenue
Amityville
NY 11701
USA

T: +1 516 546 3600
F: +1 516 546 6871
www.knittingfever.com

CANADA

Diamond Yarns Ltd

155 Martin Ross Avenue Unit 3
Toronto
Ontario M3J 2L9
CANADA

T: +1 416 736 6111
F: +1 416 736 6112
www.diamondyarn.com

DENMARK

Fancy Knit

Hovedvejen 71
8586 Oerum Djurs
Ramten
DENMARK

T: +45 59 4621 89
E: roenneburg@mail.dk

MEXICO

Estambres Crochet SA de CV
Aaron Saenz 1891-7
Col. Santa Maria
Monterrey
N.L. 64650
MEXICO

T: +52 81 8335 3870
E: abremer@redmundial.com.mx

BELGIUM/HOLLAND

Pavan

Thomas Van Theemsche
Meerlaanstraat 73
9860 Balegem (Oostrezele)
BELGIUM

T: +32 (0) 9 221 85 94
F: +32 (0) 9 221 56 62
E: pavan@pandora.be

ICELAND

Storkurinn ehf
Laugavegi 59
101 Reykjavik
ICELAND

T: +354 551 8258
F: +354 562 8252
E: storkurinn@simnet.is

**GERMANY/AUSTRIA/
SWITZERLAND/LUXEMBOURG**

Designer Yarns (Deutschland) GmbH
Sachsstrasse 30
D-50259 Pulheim-Brauweiler
GERMANY

T: +49 (0) 2234 205453
F: +49 (0) 2234 205456
E: info@designeryarns.de
www.designeryarns.de

FRANCE

Elle Tricote

8 Rue du Coq, La Petite France
67000 Strasbourg
FRANCE

T: +33 (0) 388 230313
F: +33 (0) 8823 0169
www.elletricote.com

SPAIN

Oyambre Needlework SL
Balmes, 200 At.4
08006 Barcelona
SPAIN

T: +34 (0) 93 487 26 72
F: +34 (0) 93 218 6694
E: info@oyambreonline.com

SWEDEN

Nysta garn och textil
Luntmakargatan 50
S-113 58 Stockholm
SWEDEN

T: +46 (0) 8 612 0330
E: nina@nysta.se
www.nysta.se

AUSTRALIA/NEW ZEALAND

Prestige Yarns Pty Ltd
P O Box 39
Bulli NSW 2516
AUSTRALIA

T: +61 02 4285 6669
E: info@prestigeyarns.com
www.prestigeyarns.com

FINLAND

Duo Design
Hämeentie 26
00530 Helsinki
FINLAND

T +358 50 346 0575
E: maria.hellbom@priima.net
www.duodesign.fi

BRAZIL

Quatro Estacoes Com
Las Linhas e Acessorios Ltda
Av. Das Nacoes Unidas
12551-9 Andar
Cep 04578-000 Sao Paulo
BRAZIL

T: +55 11 3443 7736
E: cristina@4estacoeslas.com.br

For more information on my other
books and yarns, please visit:
www.debbieblissonline.com